HOW TO CURE ANXIETY IN JUST FIVE THERAPY SESSIONS

HOW TO CURE ANXIETY IN JUST FIVE THERAPY SESSIONS

An Innovative Manual for Clinical Hypnotists and Psychotherapists

Dr. Patrick McCarthy

Universal-Publishers
Irvine • Boca Raton

*How to Cure Anxiety in Just Five Therapy Sessions:
An Innovative Manual for Clinical Hypnotists and Psychotherapists*

Copyright © 2022 Patrick McCarthy. All rights reserved. No part of this publication may be reproduced, distributed, or transmitted in any form or by any means, including photocopying, recording, or other electronic or mechanical methods, without the prior written permission of the publisher, except in the case of brief quotations embodied in critical reviews and certain other noncommercial uses permitted by copyright law.

For permission to photocopy or use material electronically from this work, please access www.copyright.com or contact the Copyright Clearance Center, Inc. (CCC) at 978-750-8400. CCC is a not-for-profit organization that provides licenses and registration for a variety of users. For organizations that have been granted a photocopy license by the CCC, a separate system of payments has been arranged.

Universal Publishers, Inc.
Irvine • Boca Raton
USA • 2022
www.Universal-Publishers.com

ISBN: 978-1-62734-374-9 (pbk.)
ISBN: 978-1-62734-375-6 (ebk.)

Typeset by Medlar Publishing Solutions Pvt Ltd, India
Cover design by Ivan Popov

Library of Congress Cataloging-in-Publication Data

Names: McCarthy, Patrick, 1957- author.
Title: How to cure anxiety in just five therapy sessions : an innovative guide for clinical hypnotists and psychotherapists / Dr. Patrick McCarthy.
Description: Irvine : Universal Publishers, 2022.
Identifiers: LCCN 2021052513 (print) | LCCN 2021052514 (ebook) | ISBN 9781627343749 (paperback) | ISBN 9781627343756 (ebook)
Subjects: LCSH: Anxiety--Treatment. | Psychotherapy.
Classification: LCC RC531 .M363 2022 (print) | LCC RC531 (ebook) | DDC 616.85/2206--dc23/eng/20211029
LC record available at https://lccn.loc.gov/2021052513
LC ebook record available at https://lccn.loc.gov/2021052514

DEDICATION

This book is dedicated to my wife Celia.
She is an utterly amazing woman and I am so lucky to
have had her by my side for over 41 years.

I love her so much more than she will ever know.

I have made many thousands of decisions in my life
but asking her to marry me has always been
my greatest ever decision.

Her acceptance has been my greatest ever gift.

TABLE OF CONTENTS

Preface . . . . *xi*

Chapter One
Guiding Principles of how I Conduct Therapy 1

Chapter Two
The Intake Session for Anxiety or Panic 17

A radically different and carefully planned and structured intake session that can be used for all types of anxiety without any need for discussion of the unique history of the patient! This ahistorical approach is radically different from what I was taught to do as a therapist.

The Teapot Test is a rapid expectancy generating technique masquerading as a hypnotisability test that always works.

The therapist goal of the intake session should be 'to generate hope and expectancy' so that the patient will want to return soon for another session.

Table of Contents

Chapter Three

The Second Session—The First Hypnosis Session . . . 57
   The Magnifying Glass Metaphor—a transcript. This is a conversational induction hypnosis session that can be used for virtually all patients no matter their diagnosis. It gradually and gently guides each listener into hypnosis. I've used it successfully over 20,000 times.

Chapter Four

Micro-Analysis of the Magnifying Glass Metaphor to see the Multiple Embedded suggestions that make it so effective. 71
   Every word and every pause are carefully explained.

Chapter Five

The Second Hypnosis Session—The Four Finger Technique—A Transcript. 93
   This is a technique to displace and replace unwanted, emotions, thoughts, physical feelings and images and replace them with positive ones in less than a second.

Chapter Six

Analysis of the Four Fingers Technique. 105

Chapter Seven

The Silly Voice Metaphor—The Lie Detector Exercise. . 123
   How to not believe your unwanted thoughts.

Chapter Eight

How to Think like an Optimist—The 3 P'S. 131

How to Think like an Optimist—A multi-metaphorical explanation of Attributional style and how to change it in a 30-minute session.

Chapter Nine

The Special Place of Bliss 153

The Special Place of Bliss—a technique for laying down and leaving and no longer carrying ALL emotional baggage with no need for any disclosure at any time.

Chapter Ten

Special Place of Bliss—a micro-analysis of the Special Place of Bliss to show the safety features . . . 169

Summary 187
About the Author 189

PREFACE

Dr Pat McCarthy is a great and generous friend to the British Medical and Dental Hypnosis Society Scotland and is our Honorary President...It is no surprise to me that he has written this great and generous book on how to cure patients who suffer from anxiety in five sessions. Pat, is a fellow Scot, living in New Zealand for many years and an experienced General Practitioner, a Fellow of the NZ College of General Practitioners a past president of the NZ Society of Medical Hypnosis, Member of the International Society of Hypnosis and Director and Founder, Milton H. Erickson Institute of Wellington. He is a well-qualified hypnotherapist with over 25 years' experience and 20,000 successful treatments under his belt. That makes him a force to be reckoned with and someone who thinks critically and rapidly. Pat's generalist background has meant that he has dealt with a huge range of people, from cradle to grave, ensuring that he has experience of everything affecting the human condition. This has made him challenging and fearless in his study and application of hypnosis as a healing therapy. It has allowed him to develop his own unique therapeutic style. These skills coupled with his genuine compassion for his patients makes him not only a superbly effective clinical hypnotherapist but also a charismatic teacher. His generosity to his colleagues is demonstrated in this book.

Clear effective techniques explained in a straightforward way that allows colleagues to understand and use them for the benefit of their patients. His five therapy sessions to cure anxiety not only allows his patients to disinvest themselves of debilitating anxiety but to realise their own potential for healing and personal growth. Pat wants his patients to fly away and get on with their lives free from the negativity they have been living with, often for many years, despite multiple interventions. This is not an elaborate tome that you need to decipher but a clever clear and concise description of how to treat anxiety effectively in five sessions. This book is a must have for any clinical hypnotherapist. I highly recommend it to you.

Dr Kathleen Long
MBChB MPH DRCOG
NLP Master Practitioner MBTI trained
Past President BSMDH (Scotland)
President European Hypnosis Society

CHAPTER ONE

GUIDING PRINCIPLES OF HOW I CONDUCT THERAPY

Anxiety in all its shapes and sizes and varieties, whether generalised or specific, is easily the commonest condition I am asked to treat in my role as a medical hypnotist. Anxiety and Panic now constitute over 80% of my consultations.

Anxiety and Panic are conditions I always treat with complete confidence.

I smile and I tell my patients who have a problem with anxiety I know I can help them. I want to cure them.

I say these words with great confidence as I know I have already helped many thousands of people with Anxiety and Panic over the last 26 years of practice. My confidence comes from this vast experience and the final session feedback from so many grateful patients who have told me they now feel completely cured.

If someone asks me how I seem so convinced hypnosis can possibly help them cure their anxiety or panic so rapidly, when many months or even many years of previous counselling sessions have already failed, and many other therapists have already tried a huge variety of approaches and yet have still failed to help them, I choose to reply to their quite reasonable enquiry in a very unexpected but deliberate way.

I pause and establish eye contact with them for a few moments.......... and then somewhat theatrically look up and to my right as if being very contemplative about how best to answer this question.

I then look back at them and smile.

"Let me tell you an old joke by way of an explanation to your question."

Once upon a time a very, very intoxicated man was staggering about looking intently at the ground underneath a lamp post.

A police officer saw him and politely enquired, "Are you alright Sir?"

The drunk then looked up at the police officer and replied, "No, offi-sher, I've lost my car keys and (hic).. and I can't find them... anywhere."

"You're obviously in no way fit to drive a car!"

"I know that offi-sher, I've had a few too many... drinks. A few too many whiskies. I know that.....But I still need to find my..... missing car keys."

The officer looks around at the ground—no keys are anywhere in view.

"Are you sure you lost the keys here?"

"Oh No, not at all. I lost them in that dark bush over there". Pointing in the distance.

"Then why are you looking for them here?"

"Well because there's a lot more light here under the lamp post."

Most people smile! They tend to appreciate my unusual way of answering their question.

As I said, it's an old joke, but I often use it when asked by patients to explain why I choose to use hypnosis as a treatment method and how it can potentially help. If possible, I prefer not to explain why I have chosen to answer their question by telling them the joke or even explaining the underlying message unless they specifically ask me to do so.

I thus allow them to infer the telling of the joke is indeed a very profound and indirect answer to their question.

This very unusual way to reply to their quite reasonable question is a powerful comical metaphor and conveys so much about the total futility of the types of unsuccessful therapy of looking in the wrong place, they have experienced in the past.

It also alludes to how a quite different approach from before could perhaps be extremely helpful.

Read the short joke above again and consider what the listener probably chooses to infer about me from hearing it. Would they still think I will probably be just yet another therapist trying to help them deal with anxiety in much the same old way?

I simply don't know of any faster way to allude to the huge benefits of learning to use hypnosis. Choosing to tell this joke as a reply to a serious question in perhaps even the first few minutes of meeting someone also paints me in their eyes as a bit of a joker with a sense of humour and a great degree of unpredictability and novelty.

I do not want to seem to appear to be like any other therapist they have ever encountered before who has failed to help them.

Some people however do need an explanation of the joke!

Many therapists when dealing with someone presenting with Anxiety or Panic look for answers and solutions under the light (within the conscious mind). They might decide metaphorically for instance, to conduct a systematic grid search. They might get out a large and powerful magnifying glass or perhaps increase the intensity of the light bulb. Whatever they do they will still never find the solution. The solution is not to be found under the light. We have to go to the dark bushes to find the keys.

All of these logical search actions I have mentioned above are excellent search improvement techniques.

However if you are looking in the wrong place then you cannot possibly find the solution no matter how hard you try.

Anxiety, as we all know, simply does not go way or change much at all even with better understanding, or logic, or insight or reason all of which are skills of the conscious mind.

The best way to find the missing keys is to take an element of the light (a flashlight or torch) into the dark bushes and the keys will then probably be found.

I believe the solution to anxiety and panic lies within the dark bushes (the subconscious). That is why hypnosis, that works within the subconscious mind, using tools of the conscious mind, is the best approach to cure anxiety for the root and solution to all anxiety lies within the subconscious mind.

The purpose of this book is to carefully explain to therapists, who may perhaps have little or even no experience with hypnosis, an apparently simple hypnotic rapid therapeutic solution to anxiety and panic that works and often apparently cures anxiety and panic with most of the patients I see.

The therapy appears superficially to be simple but of course it is not as simple as it may first seem.

This book is a training manual explaining the structure of my unusual and unorthodox treatment approach to cure all types of anxiety and/or panic. Anxiety is anxiety and the mechanism of anxiety is the same no matter the reason for the anxiety or the severity of the anxiety and these methods work for every variation of anxiety in almost all situations. It works for social anxiety, generalised anxiety and any somatic symptom that arises from anxiety.

In order to be innovative you cannot keep doing the same as always. Sometimes the way everyone is trained to do something is not always the best way. It's just the way it has always been done. It's the traditional way. It's what we were trained to do and what our trainers were probably trained to do. Improvements occur and they are incremental improvements but not radical. Radical requires thinking outside the box.

A good example of this is the high jump. Throughout athletic history and for hundreds of years every high jumper jumped forward over the bar whilst facing it. The most common approach was the straddle jump or scissors jump or some other forward jumping technique. High jump technique changed forever in the 1968 Olympics when Dick Fosbury utterly astonished the world of athletics by leaping backwards over the bar to win the gold medal. Media immediately dubbed this style the Fosbury Flop. This technique is now the most dominant high jump style used by high jumpers at elite level. That was a radical change.

What if there is a different way to rapidly cure anxiety. That would also have to be radical. What if we left the history component to the end or gave it little priority?

This book is not traditional therapy for anxiety. It takes a radically different approach to anxiety and panic therapy.

In a well-known movie, Forrest Gump's mother used to always say. 'Life is like a box of chocolates as you never know what you will get'.

I say people with anxiety and some other common conditions are also like a large box of chocolates. Every single chocolate in the box may well have a unique colour of shiny wrapper just as every patient has a unique personal story but underneath the wrapper you will always find a chocolate which contains cocoa, butter, sugar and a flavouring. With anxiety you will always find sympathetic overactivity, mistaken thoughts, making the mistake of believing them and pessimistic thinking. Instead of obsessing about and feeling the need to understand every detail of the wrapping I believe it is far more important to focus on negating all the common ingredients that are ALWAYS there. The wrapper (the emotional baggage) is not completely unimportant of course but what if that can always be scrunched up and discarded without even looking at it and no longer carried.

I have gone into detail to explain my specific methodology to achieve all of the above so hopefully my methods and approach (often simply referred to by my peers as The McCarthy Methods) are replicable and adaptable for use anywhere and by any therapist using hypnosis for a wide variety of conditions.

Anxiety and Panic are easily the most common conditions I am asked to treat as a medical hypnotist working in Wellington, New Zealand.

I have used hypnosis with more than 30,000 people now and with over 15,000 people who have presented with anxiety or panic, most of whom continue to tell me they are now completely cured of their previously disabling anxiety.

To clarify that statement about my experience let me be crystal clear about one particularly important issue about hypnosis from the very start.

I do not believe that I have ever hypnotised anyone!

I do not believe in the word 'hypnotise'.

Guiding Principles of How I Conduct Therapy

'Hypnotise' is a verb, a doing word. 'Hypnosis' is a noun.

I prefer to think of myself as a medical hypnotist as being like the conductor of an orchestra and the person in the chair opposite me is the orchestra which has been regularly playing some 'not particularly good music'. My words are to become the inspiration for the new music they will learn.

My job is to supply wonderful pieces of music and to be a world class conductor. The orchestra will play all the music. The conductor makes not a single note of music. The movement of the baton is silent.

The conductor obviously does not 'music' the orchestra, the yoga teacher similarly does not 'yoga' the yoga class and in the same way a hypnotist most certainly does not hypnotise. This fundamental truth about where power lies is quite different from how hypnosis is usually portrayed on TV and movies.

I facilitate people to learn how to best use hypnosis and how to hypnotise themselves.

I also do not use the term 'hypnotherapy'.

Hypnosis is an altered state of mind. Anaesthesia is another well-known altered state of mind. We do not talk about anaesthesiatherapy as we know that being in a state of anaesthesia is seldom in itself therapeutic. It is whatever skilled surgery that is specifically performed during the anaesthesia which is crucial and therapeutic.

Anaesthesia is an altered state of mind used by doctors because it allows surgical treatment which would be too difficult for the conscious mind to tolerate.

Hypnosis is an altered state of mind used by therapists because it allows psychotherapy which would be too difficult for the subconscious mind to tolerate.

It is what is specifically said in hypnosis that is crucial and not the hypnosis per se. Hypnosis is not a therapy.

Hypnosis is a means of delivering therapy. Hypnosis tends to bypass some critical awareness and doubts and so allows us to wonder.

I often say that being in hypnosis can help turn a pessimistic therapy ending "Yes But" mentality into a far more optimistic, "Why Not" mentality.

Hypnosis allows the therapy of Possibility.

What is therapeutic in either altered state is of course the content of the surgery when in anaesthesia or the specific psychotherapy content when in hypnosis.

Content is King.

That is why you will see so much focus in this book on the specific content of the psychotherapy techniques to be used before and during the hypnosis rather than on the methodology of inducing hypnosis. Words matter. They are the currency of hypnosis. The content of a hypnosis session is far more important than the experience of hypnosis.

Most of my many patients with anxiety come to me on the recommendation of their family doctors, family, or friends. Sometimes they have workmates who are very satisfied ex-patients and have already been cured of their anxiety or panic.

They know I am a medical doctor now working full time in medical hypnosis. They assume as a doctor I will be professional, competent and will practice with science, ethics, confidentiality and safety. They want to experience hypnosis and so they are a self-selected group interested in hypnosis who are more likely to be hypnotisable. Most have no experience of hypnosis.

My therapeutic goal is to help people achieve considerable improvement and even cure of their anxiety or panic in just five short sessions with me.

Most of my patients do not have comprehensive health insurance and they cannot possibly afford anything like ten or twenty sessions with me.

My patients can usually only afford perhaps just four or five sessions at most.

The financial necessity of my situation in Wellington meant when I started my practice I simply had to come up with a cure for anxiety or any presenting problem that could fit within their budget. If I only had the possibility of five sessions with someone then I would have to find a solution for each presenting problem that could be taught in just five sessions. Work apparently expands or contracts to fit the available time. Necessity is often alleged to be the mother of invention.

Each session with me only lasts approximately thirty minutes and so can easily fit within any standard hour-long session that you may have.

The five therapy sessions for anxiety includes the crucial intake session. This is the session in which the patient makes their initial assessment of me. They make an initial assessment in the first few moments with me. Initial impressions are vitally important. The intake session is the therapy session which is far less mentioned in hypnosis training. Most hypnosis training conferences I have ever attended tends to focus instead on specific hypnotic methods and techniques. The intake session chapter is easily the longest one in this book. I want to firstly explain my methodology and my goal of each anxiety intake session.

If we set out on a journey then we should obviously have a clear destination in mind. We start to move in the direction of our destination. That enables us to be more likely and able to reach the destination.

What should be the desired therapist destination of the intake session for anxiety?

That fundamental question has to be answered in order for us to direct the session in the desired direction.

Many therapists claim that every intake session they have is unique and unstructured and largely depends on what the patient brings to the session and wants to talk about. They tell me they have been trained to listen to the agenda of the patient and the patient's agenda and wishes are foremost. Most happily claim to be patient focused.

Other therapists have told me they have been trained to take a detailed history of the problem and then seek to use this information to gain some insight into the causality of the problem so they can then seek to come up with a possible plan to help that individual.

The intake session is the start of a therapeutic journey we will take with the patient and whilst the patient's goal might be to find some help for their anxiety, we as therapists have to determine what our desired goal is for the end of the intake session. If you want to know about diagnosis then you will ask diagnostic questions. If you want to find out a history then you will ask historical questions. If you want to understand severity or duration then you will ask about severity and duration. Your desired outcome for the intake session shapes the questions you ask.

Failure to set a therapeutic goal for the intake session leads to a lack of direction in questions and an unpredictable outcome from the intake session.

This first meeting or intake session should not, I believe, be simply a passive information gathering session. I will show below how much therapy can be achieved, seeded and delivered during the intake session if it is carefully planned.

I must use the intake session to create a good impression and crucially to make people become quite keen and eager to return for the next four therapy sessions that will be required to complete their anxiety cure.

I passionately believe the therapist's principal goal of a first intake session for any condition should not be the traditional history taking of the presenting problem but should be **increasing eagerness to return to complete the full course of therapy** and to **raise expectancy of success**.

I want them to return for more sessions.

People who decide to not return for the next sessions with you generally do so because they leave the intake session without enough gained enough hope their time and money will be well spent on having subsequent sessions. They have not gained enough hope that you can make a significant improvement of their problem during the intake session. You may never see them again. You will never be able to help them.

Hope of improvement of their situation is what makes people want to return to see you again.

Hope and expectancy of improvement will inevitably be raised or lowered by the structure, goal and contents of the intake session.

Perhaps the best way to have people choose NOT to return for further sessions with you is to use the intake session solely to take a detailed history of their presenting problem without also imparting the crucial hope of improvement or cure. They thus will leave the intake session feeling listened to and perhaps, to some extent, feeling understood, but without feeling hopeful enough.

I would urge you to keep a note of how many single session patients you have. How many of your patients choose not to return for a subsequent session? I keep such a note.

I lose about 2 such patients a year.

These patients are my hope failures. They are my therapeutic failures. They push me to innovate.

They are a wonderful teaching resource as they point to how I can possibly improve my approach and become even more resourceful and adaptable in engendering hope.

In order to have so many people return I must impress each new patient and to over deliver their expectations of me and of the likely content of our initial encounter before the end of this first vital session.

I believe they have to leave their intake session with the possibility and hope of having their anxiety or panic cured and not just improved.

I cannot leave this vital therapeutic aspect of impressing them to chance. Hope simply must ignite in the intake session or there might well be no further sessions.

I therefore cannot possibly let the patient dominate the content of the intake session. The intake session is far too important for merely listening to their reason for seeing me. So I deliberately and carefully choreograph the intake session, as much as I possibly can, in order to control to a large extent the content of what happens during this first session.

The intake session only lasts 30 minutes and every minute of this session must be aimed at wanting them to return for without returning for the subsequent sessions they cannot be taught and learn the subsequent 4 crucial tools to be cured of their anxiety.

I have often heard it said that 80% of a domestic paint job is the preparation stage and only 20% is the application of the paint. The better the preparation work the better the paint job. Similarly in hypnosis I passionately believe the better the attention to the detail of the intake session the better the therapy job will be. This intake session chapter is therefore unsurprisingly the longest chapter in this book. In the Stages of Change model as pointed out by Prochaska, Diclemente and Norcross behavioural change starts with Precontemplation, not yet thinking about making change. I do not see such patients. The next stage is Contemplation, thinking about change. All of my patients arrive in Contemplation stage. All of them. For every condition and issue. They would like to change but do not know HOW to change. The next stage is Preparation, that takes place during the intake session and in the time between then and the first hypnosis session. The next stage is called Action, and this begins with the first session of hypnosis and grows with further sessions. The next stage in behavioural change is the Maintenance stage and this is where they listen to recordings of the sessions. The next stage is called Termination, this occurs when they deem they no longer have the problem. That they are cured.

What follows is an accurate and detailed representation of what then happens in a typical intake session for any category of anxiety I encounter. My hope is I will impress them during the next thirty minutes and leave them hopeful and keen to come back. I have used this approach with many thousands of patients with anxiety!

I want to give you as much detail of my approach and methodology as possible.

You will, no doubt, be struck by the astonishing paucity of history taking I deem to be essential.

I do not want to appear to be like any other therapist they may have seen before. I want to surprise them and inspire them.

I want to be a welcome change.

I came to hypnosis from a background of many years as a family doctor and I grew up in Scotland, a country which has a strong tradition of marine engineering and with a strong focus on finding solutions to problems rather than simply wondering about causes. I am therefore very accustomed to treating someone without the need for a detailed history before we start therapy.

I have no need as a family doctor to take a family history when I meet someone presenting with a sprained ankle. I do not need to look at their history to diagnose and treat their acute tonsillitis. If they have appendicitis then I have no interest in any childhood trauma. I just want to make them feel well as soon as possible.

I also believe the very act of taking a classical detailed history in the intake session can have an unfortunate and negative side effect in that it can consolidate the common belief for some patients that their current state of having anxiety is the direct or indirect consequence of significant incidents from their past.

"I've been anxious ever since……."

"My anxiety began when my first child was very sick….."

Given their past is unchangeable then surely this means they cannot ever divorce themselves from their past and thus also the perception they cannot change, now or ever.

This logical conclusion of such therapeutic futility is the fundamental conundrum pitfall of any detailed history taking in therapy. They unwittingly, by relating their history, can become in their own view an unchangeable victim of their unchangeable past.

I realise I am lucky I happen to live in a country and work in a therapeutic system that allows me great freedom to choose my therapeutic approach. The Medical Council of New Zealand does not require that I as a therapist need to take a detailed history in the intake session. I can practice any way that I like as long as I am ethical, I seek to gain 10 new patients each and every week. I need to be successful in therapy and have my ex-patients sing my praises to friends and family. They are my sales force.

I have also worked in almost complete professional isolation as a medical hypnotist for over 25 years. I have no mentor and no nearby colleagues in my discipline. None at all within my country.

I am completely free to work as a therapist in whatever way I believe to be the best interest of my patient. You may not be so lucky! You may be told how you must work.

My basic approach to hypnosis is not the typical and classical medical one of 'informed consent'. It is what I call my 'fiduciary duty'. Fiduciary duty is a term used mainly in the legal profession. When you get in a cab and tell the driver you want to go to the airport then the cab driver has a fiduciary duty to get you there in the best way. The cab driver does need to tell you in advance which streets they will take.

A fiduciary duty is the highest standard of care in law. The person who has a fiduciary duty is called the fiduciary, and the person to whom he owes the duty, is typically in law referred to as the principal or the beneficiary. This fiduciary duty concept means I have to perform at my utmost to help each of my patients to assist them to achieve their goal. If that means embellishing the truth or acting or feigning surprise or fudging or entirely making up a story or metaphor or even with smokers when I resort to emotional blackmail, so be it. Not all great stories have to be true! A great story can be an effective metaphor. A great story can be a lot better than truth. Don't let truth get in the way of telling a great therapeutic story. In this case the end does truly justify the means.

CHAPTER TWO

THE INTAKE SESSION FOR ANXIETY OR PANIC

I meet my patient in my waiting room and I call out their name. This lets them know I am expecting them. I particularly like to pronounce their name properly. I am able to do this by writing their name phonetically in my appointment book when they make an appointment by telephone.

This correct pronunciation of their name is the start of the important process of attunement.

I always offer a welcoming handshake with a warm and genuine smile, whilst they are in the waiting room. Human brains have mirror neurones and most people reciprocate with a smile and a handshake of their own quite automatically. First impressions are formed in just a few seconds and I want to optimise these precious moments.

I usher them into my consulting room and there are several chairs in the room.

They are often initially not sure where I want them to sit.

I gesture to the therapy chair.

It is a truly luxurious chocolate brown leather recliner. It cost me several thousands of dollars and might be the most comfortable chair on the planet.

Clearly the most comfortable chair in the room.

"You take the good chair."

A generous offer of comfort, which is appreciated when they feel the incredible luxury of the chair as they sit down and place their feet on the footstool.

A first impression from the first few seconds of our meeting is thus created that I am both friendly and generous and exude warmth.

(Given the uniqueness and great expense of my therapy chair—it was made in Norway and imported to New Zealand and might even be the only chair of its type in New Zealand, I believe each time the patient sits in that unique and luxurious reclining chair this tends to elicit a Pavlovian-like reaction to the relaxation that will come to be associated with the extremely comfortable chair and to the sound of my soft and soothing voice. A carpenter should have the best tools and similarly a hypnotist should have a quiet office, a fabulous chair and a wonderful voice.)

I sit down in a somewhat more basic black bucket chair facing them across the corner of a large classical wooden desk and pick up a digital voice recorder. Unless the patient is really tall my seated eye level is a fraction above theirs and so they literally have to 'look up to me'. Anyone reading to this point seriously think that is just a fluke? I want people to literally and metaphorically look up to me and not down on me. They want an expert to help them. 'Someone to look up to'. Anyone also think the spacing between our chairs is not the ideal distance both for listening and respecting personal space? The lighting is dimmed and the room is always a pleasant 22 degrees. This is all subtle and subliminal communication. Communication and first impressions should be optimised. I do not have some form of OCD despite what you have just read.

"Research apparently shows we forget 50% of what we hear in just 24 hours and we forget 50% of what's left in the next 24 hrs. That's why I like to record each session and I'll give you a copy of the session so you will have the ability to remember everything that is said in our sessions."

(Virtually all patients are happy to have this service. Perhaps only a handful have ever expressed any objection in the last 25 years. I switch it to record and place it on my desk between us. Most people soon forget it is there and recording.)

This recording of the session is often very reassuring to some as it means I will not say anything strange or untoward that no one else would want to hear. It also means they will be able to concentrate fully on what I say without having to actively commit all my following words to their memory.

Given the strong evidence of the fallibility of memory I genuinely struggle to understand why any therapist who wishes their patient to remember the information they have been taught fails to record their sessions for their patients. Most of my patients nowadays already carry a sound recording device of their own in their pocket. They call it a smart phone! They could use that if they prefer.

Therapy is very much like pedagogy or teaching. We have vital psychological knowledge we want to impart to our patient. We will use each session to teach new skills and we want our patients to learn these skills. What turns teaching into learning? The concepts are related but they are not the same.

What factor is the most crucial for converting teaching into learning? Every school teacher certainly ought to know this answer. Many do not.

The golden rule of pedagogy is that it is repetition, repetition, repetition, that is the most important factor that turns teaching into learning.

How can you repeat something if you cannot fully remember what you have been told?

(Proof of the fallibility of memory—Pause for just a moment and consider how much of the little I have written so far and I'm sure you have completely understood, can you faithfully remember and repeat? I suspect you might possibly remember the dedication to my wife and perhaps you could probably retell fairly accurately the initial joke I wrote on the first few pages about the drunk man looking for his car keys, because the dedication was simple but was profound and moving and the joke was a most unusual and unexpected way of starting a therapy manual. We tend to better remember things that are completely out of the ordinary and take us by surprise.)

After writing down the basics of their name and address and how they heard about me I ask all my patients the surprising and unexpected carefully chosen signature opening question I use with virtually all my patients.

"What do you want to change?"

(This very deliberate opening question "What do you want to change?" is a quite different temporal orientation from the standard question posed by many therapists who have been trained to ask 'traditional' opening questions such as, "What is your problem?", or "What brings you here?" or perhaps "What can I do for you?" all of which ask the patient to answer by talking about their past and about their problems. I want to have them future focused and focused on finding solutions.)

The focus of a traditional standard question about the present or the past is thus on hearing about their problems and on their past.

My deliberate signature opening question asks them to talk to me about their future.

People do not come to therapy with me or to any therapist to stay the same.

People come to therapy to change......... and since all change happens in the future, I believe there is great value in being future focused on therapy producing change. This direct approach sets the therapeutic agenda precisely on the goal of change from this very deliberate opening question.

Many people I freely admit, tend to answer my unusual opening question as if I had asked the "What is your problem" question they were probably expecting me to ask them.

They often start the session by telling me about their difficulties. They also often tell me they do not want to be anxious or upset.

I suspect, if they could, they could perhaps spend the entire intake session telling me about a variety of incidents from their past if I let them.

I do not let them! That is not in their best interest. It is a matter of judgement to ascertain how best and quickly to move from listening to explaining. People vary tremendously.

I choose to spend the next few minutes writing down any key comments they make and obviously listening carefully by deliberately establishing and maintaining eye contact as much as possible and nodding and giving other verbal and non-verbal acknowledgements of understanding at key moments. I let them do most of the talking at this early stage. I listen carefully to them and am seen to be listening carefully to them. This is called active listening.

I sometimes choose to repeat a key phrase they use in a slow and spaced verbatim way with great emotional empathy in my voice and the use of facial expressions and gestures. I have been an award-winning amateur actor but it is a skill that can be learned and practised.

e.g. P. "I've not been able to get on a plane for five years and I really hate that because my daughter lives in London."

Me "So, you've not been able…. to get on a plane….. for five years…..and you really hate that…… because your daughter lives in London."

No one has ever said. "That's what I just said!"

On the contrary people often smile with relief and say, "You're the first person to really understand me." This is a further sign of attunement.

Had I paraphrased and said "So you really have a huge problem with fear of flying and your daughter is overseas" the patient would not know for sure that I had really listened and really heard them. In fact they would probably think that I did not really understand them.

When I repeat their words verbatim, it obviously means I must have listened carefully and heard and listened to every word they spoke. That careful listening is the only way I could possibly repeat their words verbatim. I echo their very own words.

The verbatim repetition is seldom consciously recognised.

Subconsciously however they realise my comments somehow perfectly reflect their own thoughts. They intuitively know I must therefore have actively listened to them and thus we start the process of them feeling understood, which I believe is far more important than simply being heard.

Patients really like knowing they are talking to a doctor who actively listens to them and understands them.

Apparently, this active listening process is not common in some therapists. You cannot actively listen and think about your next question at the same time.

My patients subconsciously infer I must therefore really understand and care about them.

After they have spoken for just a couple of minutes about the past and their problems and they know I am actively listening I usually gently stop them with a slightly raised hand gesture and a genial smile.

"My opening question was 'What do you want to change?' What do you want? You've just been telling me what you don't want. That's of course, what I find many people do.

(When you insert, with a genial smile, 'of course' they infer this response is quite normal. When you add 'what many people do' they infer their incorrect response is also quite common. This way of responding is therefore reassuring and thus not perceived as a criticism of them.)

You've told me you don't want to be anxious. You don't want to be fearful. I understand that. I do. I really do. It makes sense. You do NOT want to have anxiety. What I really want to know however is….. what you would like to be. I'd like you to tell me what you want……. using positive terms only.

If they struggle with providing an answer I often at that point add a useful metaphor. "For example, think of me for a moment as a taxi driver type therapist. A taxi driver does not really want to know where you have been or how long you have been waiting there. A taxi driver does not need to know about your past. A taxi driver also does not want to know where you don't want to go.

Telling me you don't want to go to Petone or Newtown is not much use to me. A taxi driver only wants to know where you want to go. The question of a taxi driver is always, "Where do you want to go?" An answer however like 'the airport' is a clear and precise destination and all I have to do is figure out the best way to deliver you there.

So tell me……… what you do want to change? How do you want to be different? I realise this can be difficult for some people who usually only think in terms of what they do not want. Can you tell me what you want out of therapy using only positive terms?"

(Most people I meet love hearing this simple metaphor about being a 'taxi driver therapist'. They already know taxi drivers do not need you to recite a life history about where you have been, and thus they infer I just simply need to know a desired destination. It's also good to acknowledge this task whilst sounding simple is not quite that easy.)

If we can decide on a destination we will know when we reach there. Without a clear destination how can we know when or if we have arrived?

Some people however believe they need to fill me in on lots of details about their past having presumably been trained to do so with virtually every other therapist they have ever seen about addressing their problem.

I've found with such people a rather nice way to accommodate both their perceived needs to explain their past and my needs to complete the session on time is to say.

"If you think there are some details about your past you really think I need to know in order to help you on your journey please tell me what they are. Just the bullet points of course. No need to give me all the details."

This is a delightfully quick way of giving them permission to talk briefly about their past without requiring them going into detail.

Often, I find many people are hugely relieved they do not need to go into great detail about their childhood, or upbringing or past failures or traumas.

If taking a detailed history is all that would happen in my intake session I would be surprised if many would be keen to return or be impressed.

99.9% of my patients return for subsequent sessions.

After a few attempts at goal setting and if need be, some assistance from me, we usually arrive at a therapeutic goal something along the lines of, "I want to be able to fly with calmness and peace of mind at all times."

I repeat their stated goal verbatim but slowly and deliberately." So you want to fly….. with calmness….. and peace of mind…..at all times)" I give a little nod of acknowledgement, smile, and I pause for a microsecond and confidently state still with a smile "I'm confident I can teach you how to be able to do that."

We have thus arrived at a specific positive therapeutic goal for therapy agreed with the patient and usually less than five minutes have elapsed since we first met.

Patients know they have been listened to and actively heard and agree with the stated goal of the intended therapy.

This is true attunement.

I believe they most likely want to know how I can possibly back up that extraordinary claim that would be able to incredibly change their lives.

So at this point I take over the conversation and they now listen and I start to tell them the following story with surprisingly virtually no interruption from the patient.

I become like an actor delivering a captivating soliloquy with the following intake session script that I use almost word for word with each person with anxiety or panic adding in, of course, snippets of personal details I have somehow gleaned in the opening minutes to personalise some elements to further enhance our attunement. This script is about 95% standardised and structured but it is the 5% of individualisation such as patient name and a few personal details that make it appear individualised.

"I have been attending hypnosis and psychology conferences for over twenty-five years and I find the question opener always asked about anxiety begins with the common word 'WHY'.

Why do we get anxious?

A thousand and more answers are likely to follow.

Perhaps getting on a plane, going to a dentist, entering a supermarket, giving a speech, and so on.

Sometimes for variety I've heard the opening question asked instead is another common word, 'beginning with W, WHAT'.

What makes us anxious?

The answers to this type of WHAT question are the same thousand and more answers as to the WHY questions.

The same thousands of answers goes for the other three common "W's, WHERE, WHEN and WHO."

(And so therapists using hypnosis and other methods have invented many hundreds of approaches to deal with a wide range of common fears. You can probably find some hypnotic scripts about what specific words to use with a wide variety of common problems that often generate anxiety. Scripts are available on how to use hypnosis when on a plane, or at the airport waiting at the unfortunately named TERMINAL or DEPARTURE LOUNGE or even waiting for the FINAL CALL (Oh, how I wish airport terminology were so quite different!) or at the dentist, or at an interview or a date etc.)

"It dawned on me one day that a far better question to ask about anxiety was 'HOW'.

How do we become anxious?

How many answers are there to that question of HOW?

Not thousands but in fact there is just one.

The same one HOW answer applies to each one of the thousands of WHY and WHAT reasons for anxiety.

HOW is the mechanism.

The same one HOW mechanism.

The same HOW process.

HOW is an engineering question, and if we know the answer to the HOW mechanism, we can perform reverse engineering to find the solution.

All we must learn is the HOW of anxiety and the antidote to the HOW.

(That reverse engineering antidote is what I call the cure for Anxiety or Panic and what this book will demonstrate.)

Well what is it the HOW of anxiety?

Well the answer to discovering the HOW starts with an obvious truism.

In order to become anxious we need to have a nervous system. If we did not have a nervous system we could not be anxious.

Plants, for instance, don't have a nervous system. You cannot possibly scare a bush, or a tree or a field of grass or a flower for instance.

You can of course however, scare a cat, a dog, a rabbit, a mouse, an elephant or even a lion, because all these animals like us, all have a nervous system.

Did you know we humans have two nervous systems?"

(Many people in my experience readily admit they did not know this)

"We have a central nervous system (lifting my right hand) and an autonomic nervous system (lifting my left hand).

Our central nervous system lets us raise our hand (doing so with right hand), lower our hand (doing so), put it forward (doing so), or bringing it back (doing so).

The central nervous system also lets me talk to you, listen to you and look at you.

The autonomic nervous system raises and lowers pulse rate, (lifting and lowering left hand) raises and lowers blood pressure, (again) dilates and contracts pupils, (again) increases and decreases blood flow. (again)

Raise and lower your right arm. (They do so) Easy!

Now raise and lower your blood pressure. Raise and lower your heart rate. Not so easy!

Guess which nervous system causes anxiety?

Do you reckon it is the central nervous system that we have control over or do you reckon it's the autonomic nervous system that we usually do not have control over?"

(Wait for an answer, this shows they are listening and understanding.)

"Correct! It's the autonomic. So let me explain a bit more about the autonomic."

(By stating 'let me explain' this is subtly asking permission to allow you to carry on speaking. Continuing to speak means they have given you permission to do so)

"Now the autonomic has two kinds of nerves. These are called sympathetic and parasympathetic.

If you want you can choose to think of the sympathetic as like the accelerator or gas pedal in a car and the parasympathetic as like the brake pedal."

(Notice I am offering choice!)

"The sympathetic when activated always raises the heart rate, raises the blood pressure, dilates the pupils and decreases the blood flow to the big toes.

These are the same physical changes as in anxiety.

Anxiety is always associated with sympathetic over activity. When you are anxious your heart rate is always raised, as is your blood pressure, and your pupils are always dilated and your peripheral circulation is reduced.

You cannot have anxiety and its symptoms without sympathetic over activity.

Every reason, every WHY or WHAT for anxiety produces sympathetic over activity.

Sympathetic over activity is the cause of an anxiety attack and all the symptoms of anxiety.

Sympathetic over activity is the HOW we experience anxiety.

Can you guess what parasympathetic over activity does? (Wait for an answer)

That's right. It always lowers the heart rate, lowers the blood pressure, constricts the pupils and increases blood to the big toes.

Imagine what would happen if you could switch on the parasympathetic nervous system whenever you want.

Imagine being able to slow your heart rate and loosen your muscles and slow your breathing and profoundly relax your mind whenever you want."

(Pause for a few seconds to let the enormity of this sink in)

"Sympathetic over activity (raising left hand) causes what is called an 'anxiety attack'. You've heard that phrase. Sometimes it is called the 'fight or flight or freeze' reaction."

(Many people nod at this point recognising the term)

"Parasympathetic over activity on the other hand (raising my right hand) causes what I call …….'a relaxation attack'. A relaxation attack is the opposite of an anxiety attack. (Many patients smile at this unusual and previously unheard phrase)

Imagine how your life would change if you could produce a relaxation attack in every part of your body whenever you want. (Another slight pause to allow them to imagine.)

On your next session here I will teach you, and you will learn how to produce a relaxation attack, any time you want, in less than sixty seconds.

That is a skill that would I'm sure would really change your life.

That's a great start but it's not enough."

(At this point most people in my experience are extremely eager to return to learn how to produce a relaxation attack)

"The next obvious question to ask and again it is a HOW question………… is of course.

(Saying 'obvious' and 'is of course' implies they are following the story and they are also curious and intelligent.)

HOW does the sympathetic become over active?

Well that's where the WHY and the WHAT answers come in ……………. but instead of being swamped by the thousands of possibilities…………I've discovered you can divide them all into just four categories.

The four categories that trigger the sympathetic over activity are.

Unwanted emotions—like fear,

Unwanted thoughts—oh my goodness,

Unwanted physical feelings—squirmy tummy, band around the head

Or unwanted images—failure, humiliation, dying …..or worse.

One unwanted trigger cause what we call mild anxiety.

Two triggers at the same time causes moderate anxiety.

Three triggers cause severe anxiety.

Four triggers at the same time causes what is called panic which is just intense anxiety.

How do we get rid of these unwanted categories of trigger?

Well unfortunately that's where the first problem arises. This answer took me many years to discover.

You see as well as having two nervous systems we each also have two minds.

We all have a conscious mind (raising my right hand) and a subconscious mind (raising left hand).

The conscious mind controls the central nervous system and the subconscious mind controls the autonomic nervous system.

The problem arises because the conscious mind works with language, in my case the English language.

The subconscious however works with pictures and symbols. It's basic.

If the conscious language mind thinks "I am not in Australia." The conscious mind understands the concept of NOT. It's called a negation word. That sentence means I must be in some other country.

The subconscious mind however does not understand the basic word NOT.

For instance consider what happens in your subconscious as you hear the following four sentences.

Do NOT think of a pink elephant covered in blue spots.
Do NOT think about the Eiffel Tower in Paris.
Do NOT think about the stretchy cheese on pizza.
Do NOT think about the shape of Australia on the map.

Notice how your subconscious mind gave you those four pictures almost instantly.

The word "NOT' does not work with a picture system.

It simply cannot.

Even worse, instead of getting rid of the concept it brings the concept to the subconscious mind almost instantly.

This applies to all the other negation words we commonly use.

NO, NOT, NONE, WITHOUT, LESS, NEVER, are all useless with a picture system.

So can you guess what happens in your subconscious if you think?

I do not want to be anxious.

I do not want to be upset.

I do not want to be fearful.

(Let them answer—I have been speaking a lot and this briefly engages them)

Instantly our subconscious is bombarded with the concepts of being anxious, upset and fearful.

That explains why wanting not to be anxious instantly makes us become anxious.

It is perhaps the most common mistake in thinking.

It baffles even highly intelligent people why they can decide to think "I hope I am not going to be anxious when I get on the plane", yet almost instantly their heart rate rises and they start to sweat. They do not realise the futility of NOT.

Some people have given up wanting NOT to be anxious as somehow it seems pointless and they change to something else that appears to sound more positive.

They want to be the opposite of anxious. So therefore they want to relax and be calm and be in control.

Unfortunately, what they tend to think however is.....

I want to TRY to relax. Try to calm down. Try to be in control.

'Try' is a quite common word.

Unfortunately, no matter how hard they try to relax they discover their anxiety intensifies and worsens. They often try as hard as they can to slow their breathing or try to distract themselves but they inevitably become worse and more anxious.

You may have spent a long time in the past trying to slow your breathing; trying to be positive; trying to calm down and trying to relax.

You will always fail to relax if you have such thoughts. The reason for this common failure is a simple language linguistic trap. Essentially the word TRY does not mean what you have always thought it means even throughout all your life you have probably tried your best.

What exactly does the word TRY mean?

TRY is a common word in the English language. You may have always thought of TRY as an incredibly positive word. All your life you have been told to try. You have been told to try hard, to keep trying—to try and try again until you succeed.

All though our early years I feel sure you were told to TRY your best. TRY to do well and TRY to get good results. TRY to get a good job. TRY to find a partner. TRY to have a family. TRY to have a happy life. You may have been told if you do not TRY you will not and cannot possibly succeed. That if you do not TRY then you will fail. But I contend that everything we TRY ends in failure. When there is success it is not called a TRY.

It will probably come as a surprise to learn the subconscious mind always recognises the word TRY as being a negative word. To the subconscious mind, 'TRY' means 'fail' or at least the possibility of failing.

I would go as far as to state the three-letter word TRY is the single greatest sabotaging word in the entire English language. Nor is it confined to the English language: 'TRY' has an equivalent word in every other language on the planet.

Well how and when did you subconsciously learn this? When you were just two years of age you were a bit like a language sponge. You were listening to the people speaking around you and you were learning approximately 10 new words each day. So in the space of just one calendar year you therefore learned approximately more than 3500 new words.

This was a time of your life of very rapid language acquisition in your life if you were regularly exposed to hearing language. Any parent of a three-year-old knows their child can easily talk for several hours if given a chance. They already have an extensive vocabulary.

You can have a far better and longer conversation with a child of this age than you possibly can with a two-year-old.

Let us imagine for a moment you are a two-year-old whose name is Mary. You are in the kitchen and your mummy drops a plate.

Mummy exclaims,

"Oh, Mary, I dropped the good plate and it smashed."

The first thing you hear is the word MARY. You know this is your name. Everyone calls you Mary. No one else in your family is called Mary. Not your sisters and certainly not your brother. You are the only person called Mary who is in the room.

'The good plate' simply uses three quite common and everyday words you already know as a big girl of two, having heard these three common words hundreds of times before.

Next you notice she uses the word DROPPED, a completely new word for you. You might never have heard it before.

You have certainly heard your mother say the word FELL, and you can clearly see that DROPPED and FELL look to be the same thing. The word DROPPED must therefore be just a fancy word for FELL. These words are synonyms – words that mean the same thing. You might even learn the word 'synonym' perhaps 10 or 15 years later.

From that moment on you can now choose to say your doll fell or your doll dropped. In your mind the two words become 'the same as' or interchangeable. You have now added a new word to your vocabulary.

The next words 'and it' are just two simple joining words. You already know these common words.

But the next word SMASHED is a brand-new word for you. You have never heard it before. This is hardly surprising because we do not give two-year-olds smashable toys or smashable objects.

The word SMASHED is spectacular. It is associated with a loud noise and many shards of plate flying across the floor. SMASHED also happens to be an onomatopoeic word: This means it is one of those special words that sound like what they do. Young children really love the sound of many onomatopoeic words and will often seek to memorise the word by taking in a long in-drawing of breath then repeating the word ……five times. Like this.

(I take a really deep and long breath in and point at the ground and say in a childish voice "Smashed, smashed, look Mummy smashed, bad smashed, oh smashed.)

A week later your Mummy drops another plate. This time she says 'Oh, Mary, I dropped the good plate. I tried to catch it but it smashed.'

Interestingly she says this new clause, 'I tried to catch it', in a slightly different tone of voice from the other words in the sentence. She says this clause with a slight rising inflection in her voice.

I demonstrate the rising inflection. 'Oh, Mary, I dropped the good plate, I TRIED TO CATCH IT, but it smashed.

The same rising lilt is in her voice occurs when she tells you about something good: I'll take you to the circus; I'll buy you an ice cream; let's go for a picnic; you can have a lolly…..

We use a rising inflection for good things and a lowering inflection of voice for bad things quite automatically.

(I say in a lowered inflection, you need to go to the dentist, ……..and get a little injection, ……...and eat all your broccoli.)

Your mother by using a rising inflection is instinctively telling you that in her mind she did a good thing. She made a valiant effort to catch the plate. She did not simply just let it fall but did her absolute best to catch it and to stop it smashing. She is implicitly explaining she should therefore not be criticised. She is justifying the broken plate and appealing to your sense of fairness quite automatically so as not to be blamed for the broken plate.

Your ears and conscious mind instantly hear the rising inflection and thus 'good' sound of the words "I tried to catch it'. Apparently 'tried' is therefore another example of a good thing.

But your eyes instantly see the picture of the failure to catch and the resulting smashed plate. The picture you subconsciously associated with hearing 'tried' is one of failure to catch, and thus a picture of a smashed plate with spectacular sounds and shards of china all over the floor. Tried becomes linked to the image of failure.

This is reinforced one week later when she drops yet another plate but this time she reaches out and catches it and it does not smash.

She exclaims,

"Oh, Mary, I dropped the good plate but I caught it."

When we are successful, we never say that we tried. We go straight to the verb and we say that we did.

We use the words TRY, TRYING or TRIED, depending on past, present or future tense, for times of failure or the possibility of failure.

Before you reach the age of five you will have heard your parents say TRY, TRYING or TRIED more than 1,000 times always meaning failure. When there was success you never heard them use these words.

By the time you leave primary school you will probably be exposed to the word TRY more than 10,000 times. TRY will always have the connotation of failure within your subconscious.

(I now involve the patient)

Tell me, what does this mean? "The woman went to the shop and tried to buy some bread."

(They usually answer—She was unable to buy it or failed.)

And what does this mean? "The woman went to the shop and bought some bread."

(They usually smile and say—She was successful!)

What does this mean?

"The player tried to score the goal."

(He did not.)

"The player scored the goal."

(He did.)

(This involvement of the patient lets them personally confirm how negative the word TRY is.)

I point out TRY also has a lot of linguistic cousins that essentially all mean the same thing.

Similar words are ATTEMPT, STRIVE, ENDEAVOUR, GIVE IT A GO, and DO YOUR BEST all essentially mean the same thing—fail.

Herein lies the big problem. We cannot get rid of the triggers that I mentioned of unwanted emotions, thoughts, physical feelings and images to the sympathetic nerves by using the words NO, NOT and all the other negation words and we also cannot get rid of these four possible triggers by using TRY, ATTEMPT etc.

The sabotage of the word 'TRY' is incredibly pervasive.

For instance, when a teenage girl is having sex, we will soon call her a teenage mother. She becomes pregnant! She was having sex and not trying for pregnancy!

When an older woman is TRYING to have a baby, we say that she is experiencing infertility. Every woman who TRIES to become pregnant fails to do so. The only way to become pregnant is to stop trying. Trying means failing. If she becomes pregnant, we never say that she tried. We say that she did.

Many children and even some adults really struggle to swallow pills and capsules. This is quite common. They can swallow anything else fairly easily. They can easily swallow beans that are approximately the same size and shape! The reason for this problem? Medications are the ONLY items that we put in our mouth and we hear a parent say, "Try to swallow it". Everyone who tries to swallow a pill therefore always fails.

The word TRY is the most powerful saboteur in the English language and this applies in every language.

I thought about this incredibly powerful linguistic conundrum for a long time and one day as I will explain later, I suddenly realised how to get around this problem. Essentially what we can do is produce in our conscious mind (raising my right hand to mirror the left hand) positive emotions, thoughts, feelings and images. We can use those positive triggers to displace and replace the negative ones. (I move my right hand to brush aside the left hand in a non-verbal communication of displacement and replacement)

This is the next step of the cure that will also learn in your third learning session here.

Anxiety is a two-part process caused by having a mistaken belief and making the mistake of believing it. That session will deal with the mistaken beliefs but I appreciate that some unwanted beliefs manage to get through and so I will also teach you how to not believe your mistaken beliefs. How to have a lie detector to recognise when you are mistaken. That's for another session. (Inference of several sessions)

The next HOW is of course,

HOW do we get these triggers of unwanted emotions, unwanted thoughts, unwanted feelings and unwanted images?

The answer to that question is that we think like a pessimist.

We therefore need to learn to think quite differently and the opposite of thinking like a pessimist is to think like an optimist.

Optimists are positive and look forward to a happy future. Optimists do not typically tend to get anxiety, or panic or depression. Even if they do, they can bounce back quite quickly and get back to optimism even after major issues.

I will teach you how to think like an optimist.

Think of learning optimistic thinking as like learning a simple foreign language. With a foreign language you would have to learn a lot of new vocabulary and probably several new grammar rules.

With what I call Optimese, the vocabulary is the same as that of a Pessimist and the only difference is one simple grammar rule that is easy to learn and that I will teach you. Alternatively, and perhaps even better, you could obtain a copy of 'The Optimistic Child' by Martin Seligman if you prefer to read about how to transform into an Optimist. That would give you a lot more information and at a lesser price than a session here. I'd also like you and every member of your family to read a couple of pages aloud to the others. This enables the whole family to learn at the same time and be able to discuss with the same knowledge base and permits children to be treated as equal members of the family. Shared experience is a great family bonding method. We have only been reading for a few hundred years but we have been listening for thousands of years. Our brains learn best by hearing than by reading.

The next HOW is of course, how do we grow up thinking like a pessimist?

The answer to that HOW is that we learned it before the age of five usually by listening to our parents. We learned the words TRY, NOT and SMASHED. We also learned pessimistic thinking at the same time.

Choose your parents wisely!

(Most people smile)

Now many people I say this to (thus you are not alone) think that they are most certainly not a pessimist. You might think so also.

I tend to call these people successful pessimists.

Their driving force in life is usually not fame or glory or money. Their driving force is usually fear of failure. They are often extremely hard workers who cross every T and dot every I.

They are usually successful and seldom do things unless they are sure they can succeed. They have a core of learned pessimism from childhood but develop a thin veneer of optimism and they smile and appear, on the surface, to be an optimist. However if they feel out of control for some reason that veneer of optimism slides off and the core of pessimism that they learned in childhood can suddenly explode like an erupting volcano. This explains why so many people with inherent pessimistic thinking learned in childhood do not develop anxiety till later in life when they suddenly feel out of control due to such late-onset factors such as sickness, death of a loved one, financial problems, relationship difficulties, work problems or a whole host of other possible and typical potential mid-life crises. So we have a cascade of processes that brings about all the symptoms that we call Anxiety.

a) We feel out of control
b) We start thinking pessimistically
c) We have triggers of unwanted emotions, thoughts, feelings or images
d) We believe them
e) Our sympathetic nerves get overactive
f) Our heart rate rises, blood pressure rises, muscles get tense and our mind gets anxious.

That's why you will learn over the next four sessions (inference that you will return) how to switch on the parasympathetic nerves to produce rapid profound relaxation, how to get rid of the unwanted triggers in less than a second, learn how to detect lies and finally learn how to edit your thinking from pessimistic to optimistic. Having learned these three new skills you will no longer feel helpless and out of control.

Let me further explain why I am so confident that you can be cured. (I take out a piece of paper and draw a typical mean distribution curve graph labelled Frequency on the up axis and Imagination/Hypnotisability on the bottom axis like the one below.)

[Bell-shaped curve graph with Y-axis labeled "FREQUENCY" and X-axis labeled "IMAGINATION/HYPNOTISABILITY"]

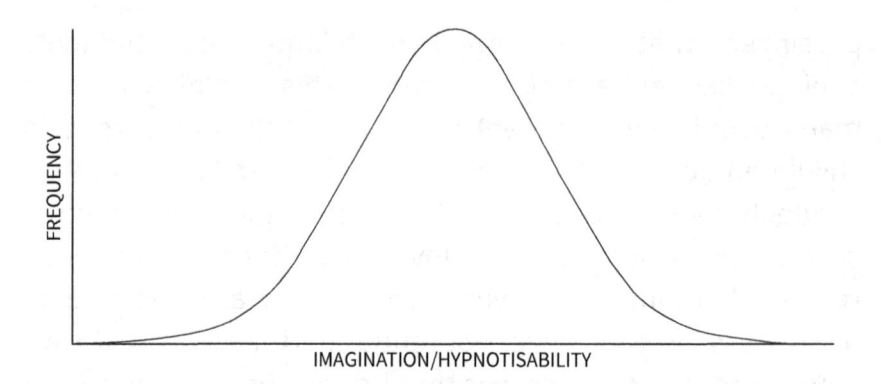

You have probably seen such a 'bell shaped curve' many times before. It is the same kind of graph that we draw for height, weight, intelligence, musicality or artistic ability. A population has, a small number of short people and a small number of very tall people. Most people are neither noticeably short nor very tall.

All normal physiological activity has a bell-shaped distribution curve: the left side represents the small number of people with extremely low scores, the right side represents the small number of people with high scores, and the centre shows the vast majority of people in the middle range.

I explain that this basic diagram is sometimes called 'the bell-shaped curve'. Many people will have seen this shape of graph many times before. It is the same shape of graph that we draw for height, weight, intelligence, musicality or artistic ability in any general community. There are for instance a small number of quite short people and a small number of very tall people. Most people however are neither short nor very tall, they are mostly of average height. In brief, all normal physiological human activity has a bell-shaped distribution curve graph resulting in a small number of people with exceptionally low scores at the left side and a small number of people with extremely high scores at the right side and the vast majority of people are in the middle range.

The vertical axis of the graph relates to frequency. The relative number of people.

The horizontal axis of the graph relates to imagination capacity and this axis also equates to their hypnotisability capacity. Hypnotisability strongly correlates with imagination capacity. In essence imagination capacity and hypnotisability capacity are one and the same.

The more imaginative someone is the more capacity they possess to use hypnosis. The more imaginative someone is, the easier they can learn to use hypnosis.

There are a small number of people on the left side of this graph.

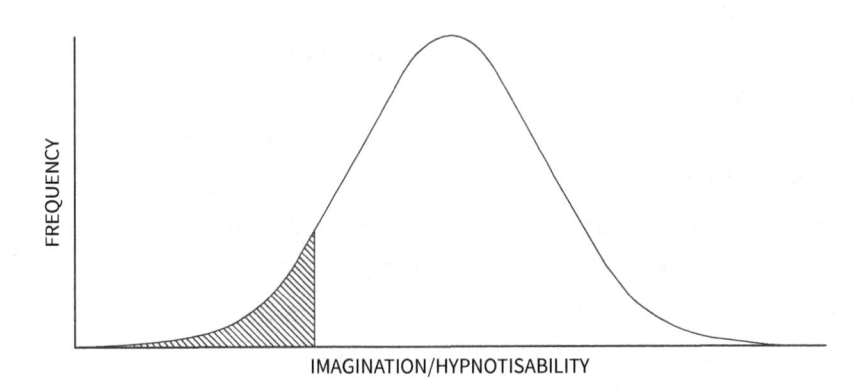

These are people with little imagination. These people are often very boring individuals and they never get much if any anxiety. They simply do not have enough imagination to lie awake for hours thinking of a whole host of things. Their logic kicks in and they stay calm without any fuss. These people seldom have enough imagination to use hypnosis and no need to learn hypnosis. We all know of some incredibly boring people who appear to really lack much in the way of imagination. I tend to call them 'accountants'

(most people smile) but when I speak to accountants I always say 'actuarial accountants' and they all tend to agree.

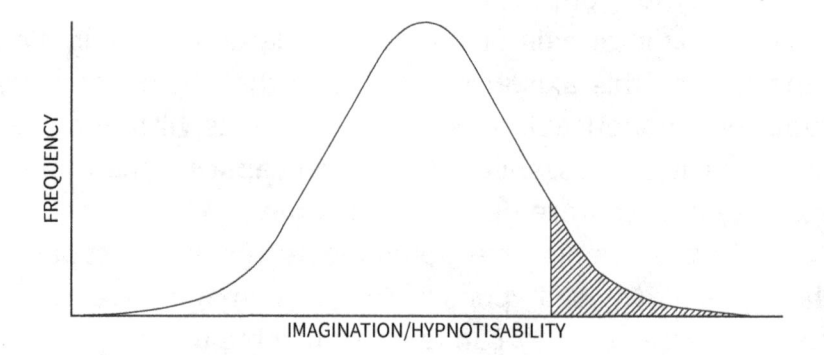

FREQUENCY

IMAGINATION/HYPNOTISABILITY

On the right side of the graph there are also a small number of people.

These are people who are very imaginative. These people at the top end of the graph can often be artists, musicians, entrepreneurs, designers, advertisers, singers or perhaps story tellers. These people are the people in our society with lots of imagination and creativity. Imaginative people however have the greatest potential for anxiety of all types. In order to be able to be anxious and thinking of all sorts of possibilities for hours you have to be imaginative. These people at the top end have the greatest imagination abilities and also the greatest capacity to use hypnosis. Everyone presenting with bothersome symptoms of anxiety therefore always has enough imaginative capacity to use hypnosis. That explains why this method is so successful no matter how severe the anxiety or how long lasting it has been.

Only the top 15% or so of people with imagination in the population have enough imagination to produce regular bothersome anxiety.

(When you have the reputation of being a hypnotist you attract patients who are interested in hypnosis and thus your self-selected patients for almost all conditions tend to be more hypnotisable than the average.)

I like to include a few notable quotes at this point.

Mark Twain once said "It ain't what we know that bother us so, it's what we think we know that ain't so that bothers us so."

Another way of describing the mechanism of anxiety is that it is "having a mistaken belief and making the mistake of believing it." So we either must stop having the mistaken belief or learn how to stop believing it. You will read later how to stop having the mistaken beliefs and, in another chapter, how to not believe them.

If I still sense any dubiety at all at this point that they will return for the next sessions I need to raise their expectancy that hypnosis will be of help to them and remove any doubt that they will be able to use hypnosis. To do so I progress to using what I call, 'The McCarthy Teapot Test.'

The McCarthy Teapot Test

This is a hypnosis expectancy enhancement procedure masquerading as a hypnotisability test.

In the trans-theoretical stages of change model identified by Prochaska, DiClemente and Norcross my patients present to me as a Medical Hypnotist at the intake session in what they have termed the Contemplation State. They are thinking about making change and wanting change to happen but have not yet committed to change. For me, the intake session is mostly about rapidly moving the patient from Contemplation to the Preparation State.

Patients approach and process each session that we have with a wide range of expectancy. In 'The Handbook of Ericksonian Psychotherapy' edited by Geary and Zeig as early in the book as just page 4 they write the following—'Expectancy is a tremendously powerful factor in the manner in which patients respond to treatment and this especially true of hypnosis. However, patient's expectations regarding hypnosis present a double-edged sword. On the positive side, favorable impressions regarding the possibilities that hypnosis can reveal in one's life add tremendous leverage to a patient's responsiveness to hypnotic interventions. On the other hand, unrealistic expectations are the worst enemies of hypnosis.'

Well, if expectancy is so all important for success in hypnosis then surely, we would want to enhance our patient expectancy if possible. We can and must do so if we want our therapy to be optimal.

We can certainly significantly reduce our patient expectancy of a successful outcome, as I have already explained, by saying, "Let's TRY some hypnosis," or "Let's give hypnosis a TRY." That would create the expectation of failure.

The following clinical technique I have used with some patients only takes a few minutes and is best used near the end of the intake session. I only use this procedure if I have a patient who is still somewhat skeptical and needs reassurance. It only adds a few minutes more to the intake session.

Let's assume the patient is female to avoid any he/she awkwardness.

Ask the patient to sit back in the chair, make herself comfortable, close her eyes and ask her to imagine that she is in her very own kitchen.

"I want you to imagine that you are picking up the kettle or jug.... and taking it to the faucet (tap).

Turn on the faucet.

SEE the water pouring from the faucet, into the kettle.

As the water pours into the kettle, LISTEN to two distinct sounds. The sound that the water makes as it leaves the faucet, and also the sound that the water makes as it fills the kettle.

Notice the kettle getting heavier with the weight of the water as you FEEL the weight of the kettle filling.

When there's enough water in the kettle turn off the faucet. Notice if the faucet makes a noise or a squeak as you turn it off, or if it is silent.

Put the kettle on to boil.

Then CHOOSE a cup.

Any cup.

It can be any size of cup, any shape, any weight and texture. It might be your favorite cup.

Or your least favorite cup.

NOTICE the shape of the handle.

It might be semi-circular shaped or shaped like the letter D or it might be more like a question mark.

HEAR the sound the cup makes as you put it down on the bench top.

Open the fridge and take out the milk container.

NOTICE the kind of milk container.

It might be cardboard or plastic, and how full it is.

It might be full, half-full or almost empty.

HEAR the sound of the warming noises coming from the kettle.

Then get out a teapot, and into the teapot, put tea leaves or tea bags, whichever you prefer.

HEAR the sound of the kettle boiling now and SEE the steam coming out of the spout.

Then, carefully, pick up the kettle and pour the hot water into the teapot.

FEEL the way the wrist moves as you tip the water in.

SEE the steam rising from the teapot.

Then put the kettle back down and put the lid on the teapot and wait for it to infuse and become ready.

Then off to the RIGHT..............SEE a bowl of fruit.

At the front of the bowl there are two oranges and a banana.

And at the back there is a lemon.

Pick up the lemon and NOTICE if the lemon is completely yellow or still has some green color.

FEEL the lemon and notice if it is a smooth shiny skinned lemon or whether the variety you have chosen is more crinkly in texture. NOTICE the shape of the end of the lemon.

Some lemons are rounded at the end, others have a little pointed bit at the end.

Then SMELL the lemon.

Notice the tangy, citrusy, lemony smell.

Then take the lemon over to a chopping board and CUT the lemon in half.

SEE the spray of juice in the air.

And SMELL the lemon more clearly more.

Pick up half of the lemon and SEE the cut, wet, glistening surface, of this juicy, juicy lemon.

Bring the lemon up to your nose and SMELL that lemon smell more clearly.

Then BITE into the lemon and TASTE the lemon juice.

Then pour some tea into the cup.

You can add milk or sugar to taste if you want. Take a sip of the tea and wash away the TASTE of the lemon.

Notice the TASTE of the tea and FEEL the WARMTH of the tea. Take another sip of the tea.

Then OPEN your eyes and let's talk about your experiences.

Post-test questions

This is the crucial part of the exercise. This requires enthusiasm and excitement from the therapist and lots of smiling and nonverbal communication of pleasure. Every reply should generate excitement no matter what the patient replies. The Tea Pot Test is perceived by the patient as a pass-fail hypnotisability assessment.

It is not!

Hypnotisability tests have passes and fails.

This test has no fails. It is a hypnosis expectancy raising procedure. Every answer is correct!

Could you SEE the things that I described?

(When they say 'yes' I smile and say something along the lines of 'visualization excellent. Well done.' Most people find that easy.)

If they say that they could not visualize this simple household scene all is not lost. Do not consider this to be resistance and a sign that hypnosis cannot work. It is so simple a visualization that complete failure has to be the patient's choice for whatever reason. I however simply do not allow failure. No one ever fails the Teapot Test unless they have the uncommon condition of aphantasia (the inability to visualise) and patients with this issue would certainly struggle with hypnosis. I have had just two extremely anxious people make such a claim and, in each case, I have still managed to be successful by stating. "Wow. That's impressive! An amazingly simple and basic memory and imagination assessment and yet your subconscious and conscious mind chose not to see those common items. Obviously, your conscious mind knows what a cup and a lemon look like of course but for some powerful reason your subconscious mind chose today to not visualize them. Amazing. That must have been really frustrating for you. It usually means that your subconscious for some reason has a powerful and strong need to be in control and not to be told by someone what to think. I'm so glad I found that out today. It protected you even though I'm sure that you wanted to see the cup and the lemon. That's really impressive defense. Your subconscious now knows that I understand and appreciate and respect that. When I teach you the type of non controlling hypnosis that I now know will help you just raise your right hand if for any reason you ever feel that you are starting to not feel or be in control. I'll stop if you ever raise your hand. (No hand has ever risen!)

Could you HEAR the sounds? The sound of the running water or the kettle boiling for instance. Did you imagine in your mind those remarkably familiar sounds?

(If they say yes then smile and say auditory excellent. Well done.)

Could you get a sense of the FEEL of the cup or the lemon, it's texture or perhaps the weight of the kettle?

(If they say yes then smile and say kinesthetic awareness excellent. Well done)

Could you SMELL the lemon?

(If they say yes then smile and say olfactory awareness excellent. Well done.)

Some people will not be able to recreate smell. I ask them if they have any nasal allergies or smell problems. If they say yes, I smile and tell them that explains why they did not get the smell easily. If they say no, I smile and state that this is the least important skill and not one that we will need to treat their problem.

Did you get the TASTE of the lemon or the tea?

(If they say yes then smile and say "gustatatory awareness excellent. Well done.")

Some people will not get the taste of the lemon but will get the tea. I smile and say "Wonderful, you were able to choose to experience the pleasant suggestion of tea and choose to discard the unpleasant one of lemon. Fabulous control!"

No matter what response they give to the modalities of visualization, auditory, kinesthetic, olfactory and gustatory I smile and explain that their answer makes them very suitable for hypnosis.

The next part of the assessment deals with dissociation proneness.

I ask them if they experienced the visualization in the first person or third person. That is, did you see your hands holding the kettle and cup or were you detached and seeing your whole body carrying out the instructions.

If they indicate first person I smile and say "Good, you were associated. Fully engaged." I explain how some other people give a different answer and how their response is the best one for hypnosis.

If they say third person detached, I smile and say," Good, dissociated, highly skilled. You automatically and cautiously used this as a defense mechanism. You saw yourself carrying out these tasks whilst you observed from a distance. **She** picked up the kettle and the cup and lemon and did the pouring, smelling and biting. So only **she** could feel these things. It's good to know that you can choose to do that because when we do the hypnosis, I don't want to teach just her the really helpful skills and end up not treating you.

The next assessment is about compliance and concordance.

I smile and ask, using a presupposition, "How did you handle the mistakes that I hoped that I made?" (Note the assumption of 'handled' and the implication that mistakes were 'deliberate'.)

Examples of 'mistakes' might be that they normally only ever put a teabag in a cup and may not even own a teapot.

The position of the fruit bowl is perhaps different from that suggested.

There may not be the specific fruit in the bowl that I suggested.

They can show concordance by, for instance, inventing a teapot, or having the teapot hover over their stove, or have a lemon in the bowl when they normally only have lemons in the fridge.

I smile and explain that even when I get it wrong, they can instantly use their creativity to cope with my story being different from their own kitchen.

If they insist on using just a teabag or resolutely have the fruit bowl in the other direction, I point out that this is non-concordance and shows that they have control and autonomy. If they don't like my suggestion for whatever reason, they are free to choose their own. I point out that if this happens in the therapy it would be helpful to point it out to me as I would not want there to be too much divergence of shared imagery.

Hopefully after this "assessment" I can state something along the lines of.

So, YOU are great at visual, auditory, kinaesthetic, olfactory and gustatatory imagination. YOU are associated which is good and you are partially non concordant for the taste of lemon. This gives me a great insight into how to deliver the best type of hypnosis that will work for YOU."

The North American version of this test is called the Coffee Pot Test.

I assume that you can imagine that script!

The Teapot Test is thus an expectancy enhancement procedure masquerading as a hypnotizability test. It improves the success of the subsequent hypnosis sessions. It takes approximately 5 minutes to administer and if carried out with theatrical gusto it adds to rapport and teamwork.

(At this point in the intake session my patients are generally quite impressed by the logic of my comments and they have raised expectancy of success if they have experienced the Teapot Test and so are usually keen to return for their first therapy session.)

I pick up the digital recorder and say "Now you know why the recording is essential. So much information to take in. That's why I will give you a recording of every session.

Now when do you want to come back and start learning how to cure your anxiety and panic?"

(Note the question I pose is not "do you want to return?" My question assumes that you want to return and the question is simply one of WHEN do you want to return.)

My final question of the intake session is "What have you learned today?"

(This final question is perhaps almost as important as my opening question of "What do you want to change". The question implies that they have been taught, they have listened, they have understood and they have learned. It consolidates expectancy by confirming learning. It is not important that they have remembered everything but crucial that they want to make another appointment. That confirms that the intake session has generated hope,)

Their answers conclude the intake session. I give them a recording of the session and invite them to listen to it again in order to remember.

Sometimes when I meet an anxious patient who has as their principal driving force in life 'fear of failure', I invite them to carry out some homework that I guarantee will make them lose this fear forever, if they wish to do so. They are intrigued and usually want to hear more. I invite them to go into 20 shops and ask for a product that they could not possibly stock. For instance going into a carpet shop and asking for a tin of red paint! Going into a butcher's shop and asking for a tie! Going into a dress shop and asking for a lawnmower! Totally ridiculous. I explain that the store assistant will probably ask them to repeat the request because they cannot believe that you have made such a request and must have misheard you. In all probability they will assume that you are insane. Can you imagine the store assistant's reaction to such an outrageous request? I explain that instead of trying to avoid failure, that this exercise embraces failure. This is spectacular failure on a truly grand scale. Worse failure that they will ever experience at any time in the future. I explain that they must act the part of a confused person who genuinely expects to find such an item. They cannot step out of character or explain that it is psychological homework. They have to endure whatever reaction comes from the assistant. That is the huge unknown. I explain that no one who has carried out this homework has ever been punched. I admit that a couple of people have been met with a few swear words. That's the worst possible reaction, could they handle a few swear words? I ask if they are brave enough to carry out the failure homework or will they just fail to do the homework. (Double bind) I explain that the people who carry out this homework tell me that it transforms their life forever and that the first store is the worst but of course it gets a lot easier after that because their expectations change. The total interaction time in each shop is less than a minute. Would they be prepared to risk a few minutes of possible humiliation and being regarded as a complete failure for the chance of a lifetime of emotional freedom?

Having used the intake session to raise their expectations of therapy, I somehow must provide a first hypnosis session when we next meet that far exceeds even these now raised expectations.

The first experience of hypnosis must be a spectacularly good experience of profound relaxation and feel amazing. That outcome cannot consistently happen with each new patient without also having a very well structured and equally well planned first hypnosis session.

CHAPTER THREE

THE SECOND SESSION—THE FIRST HYPNOSIS SESSION

'The Magnifying Glass Metaphor'

25 years ago, on a Saturday morning, I was sitting with other parents proudly watching my delighted young daughter attend her first ever ballet class. The ballet teacher was a very experienced teacher and I wondered what she would teach the students in the first lesson. She firstly taught the class how to stand in what is termed 'first position'. She explained the precise angle at which the feet should be placed and the precise position of the head, neck, arms, legs and torso. Every student was painstakingly taught to adopt the exact same posture. There was clearly only one way to achieve 'first position'. There was no place for any other variation of 'first position'. First position was the same exact position for every student. I would imagine that every girl already dreamed of one day becoming a ballerina and eventually going 'en pointe'—on her toes. They would also probably dream of one day performing a 'grand jete'—a huge leap. Firstly however, they each had to master first position. That was the fundamental basis on which every other position would be based. From first position you can learn how to transition to a demi pliet, second and third

positions and so on. But EVERY student first had to master first position. That was utterly non-negotiable.

My brain has always had the habit of taking information from one topic and applying it to a totally different other. This is the essence of what is called creativity. Apparently, creativity is not a common trait. It is the hallmark of invention and innovation. I was learning hypnosis at the same time and suddenly wondered if there could possibly be a hypnotic equivalent of 'first position'. A Hypnosis 101 if you will. A standardised and consistent first hypnosis session that would always work with everyone and with any problem. A solid foundation on which every other session would rest.

I had been trained that therapy ought to be individualised and that the content would obviously depend on the presenting patient. It should therefore never be scripted. Each initial session of hypnosis would therefore always be different and the therapy skill of the therapist was how to creatively choose the content that best spoke to the patient. That would require extremely creative therapists. But these are uncommon. These are the maestros we see at international conferences who seem to be able to always produce the perfect set of words. What, would be the result however, if I could make 95% of the first session standardised and scripted, allowing just 5% for some creativity and individualisation such as using their name or referring to their occupation. That would completely turn the method of therapy on its head and mean that we could plan and hone and optimise the vast majority of the first hypnosis session in advance ensuring well-planned content, yet somehow with just a few key phrases make the recipient feel that the standardised session was personalised to them. Was such a session possible? That was my goal. I sat down and composed such a session and refined and edited it over many years till it is now in what I consider to be the finished state.

I use this technique that I call 'The Magnifying Glass Metaphor' with over 99% of my patients as the first session of hypnosis with my patients no matter what condition they present with. This approach is their introduction to clinical hypnosis and it predictably and reliably always produces a wonderfully comfortable state of hypnosis in virtually each and every listener who chooses to follow the instructions. I have delivered a version of this same technique more than 30,000 times so far, yet each listener hears it for the first time. I never get tired of using it because every listener is a new patient, just as a ballet teacher presumably never tires of teaching first position to a newcomer.

The session can be delivered in approximately 30 minutes.

As you will soon discover it also contains over 300 embedded direct and indirect suggestions.

I passionately believe that the very first experience of hypnosis that any patient experiences must ideally be a genuinely great one. Such an outcome must not be left to chance if you want them to desire to return for further sessions.

I welcome each patient and usher them again to the luxurious therapy chair.

I ask them to briefly tell me what they remember from the last session.

I nod and complement them on each item that they remember and always smile.

I then move quickly into teaching them hypnosis.

I have written out the entire script that I usually use. Perhaps 95% of this script will be used with every patient irrespective of their reason for attending but the remaining 5% should be tailored to the specific individual based on the small clues they have provided in their brief earlier comments during the intake session.

I believe it could be educationally useful as you read the script below to consider why I have chosen to use the exact words that I do.

Remember that virtually all the words that I have carefully chosen are there for a reason.

I have laid the script out sentence by sentence to show the best cadence with which it should be delivered.

Pause very briefly after each sentence.

This chapter simply provides the content of the session so that it is easy to read out to a patient but I believe that a curious therapist would surely like to uncover the micro structure of the session rather than simply have the answers given at this stage.

You will most probably likely miss many of the hundreds of embedded suggestions that are contained in this metaphor so I have provided the subsequent chapter that supplies the detailed information about the reasons behind why I have carefully chosen each word.

Magnifying Glass Metaphor

"Firstly, let me explain what hypnosis is like.

It's not like what you might have seen on TV or stage shows.

There are no swinging watches.

It's nothing like that.

It is more like listening to a play on the radio.

And because it's radio it's my job to tell the story and it's your job to imagine the scenery that my words create in your imagination.

So let me explain the storyline of the play.

I'll start by talking about the room, then I'll get you to focus in on the body.

Then I'm going to branch off and tell you a little story from my childhood that you may or may not relate to your own childhood.

Then I'm going to get you to focus all through the body and then you can tell me what feels different about the body.

So just make yourself comfortable and start by just closing the eyes and take a few relaxing breaths, whatever that expression means to you.

And just listen to the sound of my voice.

Now at all times you can be aware of your surroundings.

Notice how even with the eyes closed you can still be aware of the size and shape of the room; you can know where the door is and how far apart the chairs are.

You can hear noises, perhaps traffic noises.

You can feel fabric under the fingers, you can notice if the fabric is rough or smooth, shiny or dull.

And all of these things that I have mentioned so far are all examples of what's called external awareness.

Awareness of our surroundings.

We spend most of our life externally aware.

But today you're going to learn about what's called, internal awareness.

Now internal awareness comes in two varieties.

Positive and negative internal awareness.

Negative is the most common one, the one we all know about. For instance if we get a tummy pain, we tend to focus in on it. We notice the site of the pain, whether it's top, middle or bottom and whether it's left or right or central.

Then we notice the severity, whether it's mild, medium or severe. Then we start jumping to conclusions about the significance.

Is it constipation?

Is it a dodgy pie I had at lunch?

Is it the start of appendicitis ………? or something much worse?

And you know what it's like when we get unwanted thoughts, perhaps anxiety or fear or

a) (How can I get in a lift?)
b) (When will I ever be calm?)
c) (How will I ever get on a plane?)
d) (How could I ever be ok with needles?)

And how these thoughts can sweep aside logic, common sense and reason and leave us feeling helpless and hopeless, but on the other hand, there's what called positive internal awareness.

Now not many people know about positive internal awareness because it requires focused concentration.

And I'm lucky because I first learned about the power of focused concentration more than fifty years ago.

Back in those days I was quite young and I lived, believe it or not, in a place called Scotland.

And on one of those really, really hot days that took place in that brief couple of weeks that we lovingly called the Scottish summertime I used to enjoy playing with a magnifying glass.

You see, my father owned an industrial strength magnifying glass, on a stand.

He used it for his hobby of repairing watches.

And when he wasn't looking, I would borrow the magnifying glass and sneak it outside under my jersey with a piece of newspaper.

Often, I would have my little sister/brother with me.

I've always been a bit of a show off.

Well…. You can imagine what my little sister/brother was like.

"You're not supposed to have that.

I'm going to tell on you.

You'll get into terrible trouble."

And I would say "Shooosh!"

But instead of holding the magnifying glass up close to the paper to magnify the print I held it at a distance.

You can probably imagine what my sister/brother said.

"That won't work.

That's too far away.

That won't magnify the print."

Till she/he suddenly saw how the light from the sun was passing through the lens, and because of the very special shape of the lens.

Well I bet you know what happened.

See how the light focused all the way down to this tiny, tiny dot of incredibly bright white light.

And then, the white dot started to become brown, and it darkened, and it smouldered and it smoked till suddenly it burst into flames!

And my sister would say "Wow, can I do that?"

So I taught her how to do it.

I taught her that you had to hold it at just the right distance. Not a millimetre closer nor further away.

Just the right distance.

Secondly you had it to hold it really still.

Totally focused on that one spot and only that one spot till it changed.

Now back in those days that was focused concentration of light and heat energy from the sun, which I'm told is approximately 150,000,000 kilometres away.

But today after that brief introduction, you are going to learn how to take the power of your powerful positive subconscious creative imagination and I'm going to show you how to focus that power by using your conscious logical thinking mind like a really powerful magnifying glass used as a focusing tool to be able to focus on just one thing and make that one thing the.............right foot and toes.

Focus all your thoughts, your concentration and every scrap of your awareness onto the right foot and toes.

And only the right foot and toes.

As you do so.

Feel the foot change.

When I say change it might tingle or twitch or might just become floppy.

Then focus on the right lower leg, particularly around the back, cos that's where all the muscles are.

Then focus on the right upper leg, and because the thigh muscles are bigger and longer it's usually easier to feel the softness and looseness.

Now focus all your attention on to the left foot and toes.

Feel whether it moves a fraction and if so in what direction it moves.

Or whether it just feels nice and floppy.

Then focus on left lower leg.

I wonder if you can feel the muscles under the skin.

Then focus on the left upper leg.

Pay attention to the loss of tension.

Now people have often said to me that this slow steady way of guiding you into muscle relaxation and eventually into what's called hypnosis is a bit like watching a piece of wax start to melt.

At first the wax starts off solid and white, but as I start to speak in my soft and gentle voice, and particularly if at

The Second Session—The First Hypnosis Session

any stage the eyelids flicker or twitch, the wax starts to soften and to melt.

Oh, initially, the wax still seems to be the same, at least on the outside.

That's because it's melting from the inside, till suddenly it becomes soft and softening till eventually it becomes clear and runny and quite liquid.

So that now as you focus on the buttocks and pelvis you can notice what I mean by soft and softening from within.

Then as you focus on the tummy muscles, feel the slow steady rise and fall in time with the breathing.

Speaking of the breathing, as you focus on the muscles of the chest, I'm sure you will have noticed that the breathing is now much slower and far more relaxed.

I wonder if you've noticed yet that it's the out breaths in particular that are allowing you to become even more relaxed with each and every out breath.

So as you focus now on THE shoulders you can feel the easy rise and fall in time with the breathing.

Now I want you to really sharpen up your focus as much as you can and focus all of your attention onto the right upper arm.

Feel it just hanging there now, by the side of the body, loose and floppy, like a piece of cooked spaghetti.

Now focus all your attention onto the right lower arm.

I wonder if you can feel the muscles loosening under the skin, under the sleeve.

Now focusing in on the right hand and fingers.

Feel inside each knuckle, every tiny little joint till it's just the shape of the bones holding the hand in place.

Now shift the focus to the left upper arm.

Floppy as.

Now focused on the left lower arm.

Just hanging there.
And the left hand and fingers.
Every knuckle, every joint.
That's good.

Now shift the focus up to the big neck muscles and because of the sheer weight of the head, all 5.4 kg of it, it might perhaps move a fraction, to a position of absolute rest or just stay quite still and rested.

Now focusing in on the chin and jaw.
Feel it relaxing from the inside to the outside.
Then focusing in on the cheeks.
Somewhat droopy and floppy.
And then the eyelids, which have so patiently waited their turn.
Feel them closed now, like shutters on a window.

And just when you might think that the eyes couldn't possibly close any more, notice how the little muscles at the sides of the eyes let go and perhaps with a final flicker the eyes are now completely closed.

So now as you focus on the forehead.
Feel it relaxing, smoothing and soothing away.
And the top of the scalp and the back of the head.

So that now and with every slow breath that you take out, you can feel a sort of ripple of relaxation flowing through the body, with each and every out breath.

And this is what I call light hypnosis.

Notice how in light hypnosis you can still of course have the external awareness as promised.

You can still know the size and shape of the room.

You can still hear any noises and you can still feel the fabric of the clothes.

But I hope you can now appreciate the vastly increased positive internal awareness.

How the mind has modified the muscles and how the body has responded to the brain.

You'll be able to speak quite easily.

So tell me, in your own words, what do you notice the body feels like now?

So tell me.

What do you notice about the weight of the body now?

What does it feel like?

Now obviously you know logically that the body cannot be any heavier/lighter than when we started.

Do you want to know why it feels that way?

Well for the first time in your life, every muscle fibre in the body, and that's well over 400 million of them, is totally and completely relaxed.

And when they all signal this back to the brain at the same time, then the brain understandably gets swamped and mistakenly conclude that the body is now incredibly light/heavy.

That's excellent.

Well done.

And tell me.

What do you notice now about the temperature of the body?

If client says WARMER

Well that interesting.

The temperature of this room is about 20 degrees

The temperature of your body is 37 degrees.

How can a body of 37 degrees get warmer in a room of 20 degrees?

That defeats the laws of physics.

The body has a thermostat that keeps the body at 37 degrees.

It doesn't change.

However the skin temperature can change quite a lot.

When we are worried or anxious our skin becomes cooler.

When we are terrified, we can break out in a cold sweat.

So of course when we are profoundly relaxed the skin is always warm and dry.

If the client say COOLER Say "Well done, you know that the body temperature stays constant.

Now you probably know where the phrases "Chill Out" or "Keep Your Cool" or "Cool It" comes from.

And tell me.

I know this is somewhat bizarre.

What does the brain tell you has happened to the size and shape of the body?

That's right.

It does feel bigger/smaller/wider/ blobbier.

Now you can know what I mean by melted wax.

So correct me if I'm wrong.

But you have just changed your perception of body size, shape, weight and temperature and become incredibly relaxed.

True?

Well that's amazing because I never asked you to change any of these things.

I just told you a story of two naughty children playing with a magnifying glass and then I asked you to focus on each part of the body.

The word that I used was the word focus.

I have no recollection of asking you to become heavy/ light, warm/cool, big/small.

Would you like to learn how to be able to reproduce this amazing state of relaxation any time that you want in less than sixty seconds?

Everyone always says "Yes".

I think we both know why.

So let me bring you of out of hypnosis in order to teach you self-hypnosis.

I'm going to simply count from 1 to 10

When I reach the count of 8 the eyes will open, spontaneously all by themselves and at 10 you will be fully awake and back to reality.

And if for any reason, you are interested.

You can notice what happens if you try to open the eyes before the count of 8.

1, 2, 3, 4, 5, 6, 7, 8 eyes open 9, 10

3 options happen.

1 Opens eyes. "Excellent that proves you are in control. You need to know that."

2. Does not bother. "That's fine. You don't have to try."

3. Eyes cannot open. You probably thought I said you would not be able them, but all I said was notice what happens if you try to open them. Try means fail to the subconscious as I told you already. That's why you are doomed to fail if you listen to the word try.

Now would you like to learn how to reproduce that same feeling of great relaxation any time that you want in less than 60 seconds?

Let me show you.

Now for some Self-Hypnosis.

Take your hands and place them palms together in a typical 'prayer-like' position.

Then fold the fingers over till the finger tips are touching the knuckles of the other hand.

Then extend the index fingers to as near parallel as possible.

Then simply stare at the gap between the fingers.

Feel the fingers being drawn together by the power of the subconscious.

Drawn together like magnets.

When the fingers touch…….. just close the eyes.

Take a deep breath in and as you breath out go right back into hypnosis.

Notice how good that feels.

Now just count to ten inside your head and at eight the eyes will open.

Excellent!

Now I want to prove that all hypnosis is self hypnosis so now I want you to repeat what I have just shown you and I will say nothing.

Excellent.

Next session, I'll teach you how to get rid of all the unwanted triggers.

CHAPTER FOUR

MICRO-ANALYSIS OF THE MAGNIFYING GLASS METAPHOR TO SEE THE MULTIPLE EMBEDDED SUGGESTIONS THAT MAKE IT SO EFFECTIVE

This chapter explores and explains the multiple direct and indirect suggestions that make the experience of the listener so predictably wonderful. In addition to the actual words I'd also like you to consider the intonation and if this is particularly crucial, I have underlined the specific words that should be vocally stressed. You may also be aware of other suggestions that you find embedded such as repetition of key phrases.

THE MAGNIFYING GLASS METAPHOR

Firstly	These are thus just preparatory comments so this is not yet the actual hypnosis. Using this word reduces any potential pre-existing anxiety about the hypnosis
Let me	Means give me permission
Explain	Means make clear and i have your permission to do so

What hypnosis is like	Note not what hypnosis 'is'—i say, 'is like' thus i'm using a simile
	Now a not set coming up
	3 Negations - not, no, nothing
It's <u>NOT</u> like what you might have seen on TV or stage shows.	Of course not!
There are <u>NO</u> swinging watches.	Don't be ridiculous!
It's <u>NOTHING</u> like that.	So what is it then?
It is more like	Another simile
listening to a play on the radio	
And because	Truism
It's radio	Respective roles and duties
It's <u>MY</u> job to tell the story,	
And it's <u>YOUR</u> job to imagine the scenery	Visualise
That MY words create	Inference of impact
In YOUR imagination.	You are the orchestra
So let	Give me permission to speak
Me explain the storyline of the play.	Almost a repetition of the first line
I'LL start by talking about the room, then I'LL get YOU,	Directive but very subtle
To focus in on THE body,	Note the use of the direct article word "the" rather than using your—this helps to promote dissociation
Then I'm going to branch off,	Apparently this section will not be part of the therapy

And tell you a little story from my childhood,	Diminutive and trivial
That you may	Permissive
Or may not	Bind of all alternatives
Relate to your own childhood	Allusion to an upcoming age regression suggestion
Then I'm going to get you	Directive
To focus all through THE body and then you can tell me what feels different	Presupposition of change
About THE body.	Now comes my favourite line
So	My favourite segue word to link to a new concept
Just	A lovely casual effortless word
Make	You do something to change
Yourself	Your job
Comfortable.	Supposition that this is an easy change
And start,	Start what? The hypnosis?
By just closing THE eyes	Direct instruction—the super rapid and seamless conversational induction
And take a few <u>relaxing</u> breaths,	Any type of breaths will be relaxing
Whatever that expression means to you,	It's ok to not know exactly how to take relaxing breaths
And just listen to the sound of my voice	Direct command suggestion

	Now comes a yes set-multiple mental 'yes' truisms followed by a helpful suggestion that is accepted due to the momentum of agreement
Now at all times you can be aware of your surroundings	Y
Notice how even with THE eyes closed you can still,	But might not be later?
Be aware of the size and shape of the room,	Y
You can know where the door is	Y
	Visualise
And how far apart the chairs are.	Y
You can hear noises,	Y
Perhaps traffic noises.	Y
	Auditory
You can feel fabric under THE fingers,	Y
You can notice if the fabric is rough or smooth,	Y
Shiny or dull.	Y
	Kinesthetic
And all of these things that I have mentioned so far, are all examples of what's called external awareness	Y
Awareness of our surroundings.	Y
We spend most of our life externally aware.	Y

But today you're going to learn about what's called, internal awareness.	Positive helpful suggestion
Now internal awareness comes in two varieties. Positive and negative internal awareness.	Sounding like yet another truism
	Another yes set
Negative is the most common one,	Y
The one we all know about.	Y
	It is common
	Knowledge to everyone
For instance if we get a tummy pain,	Not using abdominal- tummy is more informal
We tend to focus in on it.	Y
We notice the <u>Site</u>	Stress this
Of the pain,	Y
Whether it's top, middle or bottom	Y
And whether it's left or right or central	Y Binds of all alternatives
Then we notice the <u>Severity</u>,	Stress this Y
Whether it's mild, medium or severe.	Y
	More binds of all options
Then we start jumping to conclusions about the <u>Significance</u>.	Stress this Y
Is it constipation?	

Is it a dodgy pie I had at lunch?

Is it the start of appendicitis ....?

Or something much worse?	Even more binds of all options
And you know	TRUISM
What it's like when we get unwanted thoughts, perhaps anxiety or fear or.	
	Insert the specific reason for the anxiety consultation
	e.g a) (How can I ever get in a lift?)
	b) (When will I ever be calm?)
	c) (How will I ever get on a plane?)
	d) (How could I ever be ok with needles?)
And how these thoughts can sweep aside logic, common sense and reason	Y
And leave us feeling helpless and hopeless	Y
BUT, on the other hand, there's what called positive	Stress this
Internal awareness.	Positive suggestion
Now not many people know about positive internal awareness because it requires focused concentration.	Not many people know so thus you today are really lucky
And I'M really lucky	Just in case you missed the inference of luck
Because I first learned about the power of focused concentration more than	Pause

Micro-Analysis of the Magnifying Glass Metaphor

Fifty years ago.

                Invitation to age regress

Back in those days I was quite young

                Duh

And I lived, believe it or not, in a place called Scotland.

                Comedic pause 1

                This is gentle humour—my accent is indeed very scottish so it is not at all hard to believe.

                If, however, you do not have a scottish accent then obviously if reading this aloud do not use these actual words.

                Now some gentle humour about scottish weather

And on one of those really, really

                Emphasis by repetition

Hot days that took place in that ……

                Comedic pause 2

Brief couple of weeks ………that we lovingly called…… the Scottish summertime.

I used to enjoy playing with a magnifying glass.

You see, my father owned an industrial strength magnifying glass, on a stand.

                The listener invariably on hearing the unusual expression "industrial strength" translates it as meaning 'big and powerful' that internal inference of power is far better than my using those words.

He used it for his hobby of repairing watches.

                Mere persiflage—verbiage to add an air of authenticity

How to Cure Anxiety in Just Five Therapy Sessions

	Now use a conspiratorial hushed voice
And when he wasn't **looking**	
I would **borrow** the magnifying glass	
and **sneak** it outside	
Under my jersey	
With a piece of newspaper	
	Emphasise the words in bold
Often I would have my little sister (brother) with me.	Use 'sister' if talking to a female patient. Use 'brother' if talking to a male patient. This enhances the role plays.
	This is also a further indirect suggestion to induce age regression
I've always been a bit of a show off	Self deprecatory comment which distracts from the preceding suggestion of naughty conspiracy
Well….	
You can imagine what my little sister/brother was like	
	Direct suggestion to age regress and visualise
	Now adopt a childish voice
"You're not supposed to have that.	
I'm going to tell on you.	
You'll get into terrible trouble."	

78

Micro-Analysis of the Magnifying Glass Metaphor

	Back to normal voice
And I would say "Shooosh!"	
But instead of holding the magnifying glass up close to the paper to magnify the print I held it at a distance.	
You can probably imagine what my sister/brother said.	
	Childish voice again
"That won't work. That's too far away	
That won't magnify the print."	
	Back to normal voice
Till she/he suddenly saw how the light from the sun was passing through the lens, and because of the very special shape of the lens.	
Well I bet you know what happened.	This enhances collaboration
See	Visualise
How the light focused all the way down to this tiny, tiny dot	Really focused
Of incredibly bright white light.	Alliteration
And then, the white dot started to become brown, and it darkened, and it smouldered and it smoked till suddenly……. It <u>burst</u> into flames!	'Burst' said with some excitement
And my sister would say "Wow, can I do that?"	Even more excitement and in a childish voice
So I taught her …… how to do it.	I am a teacher and you are a learner

I taught her that ………. you had to
hold it…

                                        Ideally saying 'hold' at the top of in breath to induce a slightly held breath and thus catalepsy

At just the right distance.

Not a millimetre closer nor further away.

Just the right distance.

Secondly, you had it to hold it ….. really still.   Further catalepsy suggestion

Totally focused on that one spot ….. and only that one spot till it changed.

Till it trans formed   It trance formed

                                          Truisms

Now back in those days that was focused concentration of light and heat energy from the sun,   Y

Which I'm told is approximately 150,000,000 kilometres away.   Y

But today.   Stopping the age regression

After that brief introduction   Now is the time that the 'hypnosis' apparently starts!!!

You are going to learn   Promise

How to take the power of your powerful positive subconscious creative imagination   Said like a truism and very complimentary

Micro-Analysis of the Magnifying Glass Metaphor

And I'm going to show you how to <u>focus</u> that power by using your conscious logical thinking mind like a really powerful magnifying glass <u>used</u> as a focusing tool to be able to focus on just <u>one</u> thing,

and make that <u>one</u> thing THE

    Again using 'the' rather than 'your' promotes dissociation

Right foot and toes.

Focus all your thoughts, your concentration and every scrap of your awareness onto THE right foot and toes. And <u>only</u> THE right foot and toes.

As you do so.

<u>Feel</u> THE foot change.	Kinesthetic and dissociative
When I say change …… IT	Dissociative
Might tingle or twitch, or might just become floppy.	Bind of comparable options
Then focus on THE right lower leg, particularly around the back, cos	A colloquial nz linguistic contraction of 'because'
That's where all the muscles are.	Truism
Then focus on THE right upper leg, and because	Bind
The thigh muscles are bigger and longer	Truism
It's usually	But not always
Easier to feel the softness and looseness.	Assumption

Now focus all your attention onto THE left foot and toes.

Feel whether IT moves a fraction and if so in what direction IT moves. Or whether IT just feels nice and floppy.	Bind of two alternatives
Then focus on THE left lower leg. I wonder if you can feel THE muscles under THE skin.	
Then focus on THE left upper leg. Pay ATTENTION to…… the loss of TENSION.	This uses a homophone
	Now inserting an amnestic loop metaphor that has a suggestion of state change. The amnestic loop metaphor is seldom remembered at the end of the session but the imagery contained is useful to reach the desired outcome of profound floppiness
Now people have often said to me	This is common
That this slow steady way of guiding you into muscle relaxation	First use of the word relaxation
And eventually into what's called hypnosis	You are not necessarily there yet
Is a bit like watching a piece of wax starting to melt.	Metaphor
At first the wax starts off solid and white, but as I start to speak in my soft and gentle voice, and particularly if at any stage THE eyelids flicker or twitch, the wax starts to soften and to melt.	If they do flicker, then i insert 'like that'
Oh, initially, the wax still seems to be the same, at least on the outside.	Insert slight snort of derision for doubters that the body is changing

That's because	Powerful reason
It's melting from the inside, till suddenly it becomes soft	Noun
And softening	Process
Till eventually it becomes clear and runny and quite liquid.	Exit the amnestic loop leaving behind the imbedded state change suggestion
So that now as you focus on THE buttocks and pelvis you can notice	Gentle suggestion
What I mean by soft and softening from within.	Linking back to the amnestic loop suggestion
Then as you focus on THE tummy muscles,	Again not using abdominal
Feel the slow steady rise and fall in time with THE breathing.	
Speaking of THE breathing, as you focus on the muscles of THE chest I'm sure	I am confident
You will have noticed	Will rather than can
That the breathing is now	It has changed
Much slower and far more	It has changed
Relaxed.	Second use of relax
I wonder if you've noticed YET	You already have noticed or later will, but you will notice.
That it's THE out breaths in particular that are allowing you	Interesting use of allowing
To become even more relaxed	3rd use of relax
With each and every out breath.	Breathing out is increasing the relaxation

How to Cure Anxiety in Just Five Therapy Sessions

So as	Do two things at once
You focus now on THE shoulders you can	Gentle suggestion
Feel the easy rise and fall in time with THE breathing.	Truism
Now I want you to really sharpen up your focus	Suggestion of increased focus
As much as you can and focus all of your attention onto THE right upper arm.	
Feel it just hanging there now, by the side of the body, loose and floppy, like a piece of cooked spaghetti.	Kinaesthetic suggestion of looseness
Now focus all your attention onto THE right lower arm.	
I wonder if you can feel THE muscles loosening under THE skin, under THE sleeve.	
Now focusing in on THE right hand and fingers.	
Now focusing in on THE right hand and fingers.	Don't they always!
Now shift THE focus to THE left upper arm.	
Floppy as.	Another friendly nz colloquialism. The common unfinished simile. I let the client mentally finish that sentence in any way they wish.
Now focused on THE left lower arm.	
Just hanging there.	
And THE left hand and fingers.	

Micro-Analysis of the Magnifying Glass Metaphor

Every knuckle, every joint. That's good.	Reassurance of doing well
Now shift THE focus up to THE big neck muscles and because of the sheer weight of THE head, all 5.4kg of it,	Truism
	Say 12lb if talking to someone who still uses imperial measures
Might perhaps	Or may not
Move a fraction, to a position of absolute rest	Total
Or	
Just stay quite still and rested.	Bind of two wonderful possibilities of outcome
Now focusing in on THE chin and jaw. Feel IT relaxing	Process
From THE inside to THE outside.	Does it really?
Then focusing in on THE cheeks.	
Somewhat droopy and floppy.	
And then THE eyelids, which have so patiently waited their turn.	Eyelids are patient?
Feel them closed now, like shutters on a window.	Metaphor
And just when you might think that THE eyes couldn't possibly close any more, notice how THE little muscles at the sides of THE eyes let go	
And perhaps with a final flicker THE eyes are now **completely** closed.	
	This will become useful later.
So now as you focus on THE forehead.	

Feel it relaxing,	Next use of relaxing
Smoothing and soothing away.	
And the top of THE scalp ….and the back of THE head.	
	Let the listener insert the missing verb—relaxing
So that NOW and with every slow breath that you take out, you can feel a sort of ripple of relaxation flowing through the body, with each and every out breath.	
And this is what I call light hypnosis.	
	Wow—if this is merely light hypnosis it is astonishing
Notice how in light hypnosis you can still of course	To allay any doubt
Have the external awareness as promised.	Y
You can still know the size and shape of the room.	Y
You can still hear any noises	Y
And you can still feel the fabric of the clothes.	Y
But I hope you can now appreciate	Double meaning of appreciate
The vastly increased positive internal awareness.	Positive suggestion
How the mind has modified the muscles and how the body has responded to the brain.	Alliteration

You'll be able to speak quite easily	Vocalisation facilitation suggestion
So tell me, in your own words	Tautology—whose other words would you use
What do you notice the body feels like now?	
	Presupposition of change
	Whatever the client says—state "that's right!"
So tell me. What do you notice about the weight of the body now? What does it feel like?	Whatever the client say—state "that's right, well done."
Now obviously you know logically that THE body cannot be any heavier/lighter than when we started.	
Do you want to know why it feels that way?	
Well for the first time in your life, every muscle fibre in THE body, and that's well over 400 million of them, is totally and completely relaxed. And when they all signal this back to THE brain at the same time, then THE brain understandably gets swamped and mistakenly conclude that THE body is now incredibly light/heavy.	
That's excellent.	
Well done.	
	The result was their success
And tell me. What do you notice now about the temperature of THE body?	

Well that interesting. The temperature of this room is about 20 degrees

The temperature of your body is 37 degrees. How can a body of 37 degrees get warmer in a room of 20 degrees? That defeats the laws of physics.

The body has a thermostat that keeps the body at 37 degrees. It doesn't change

However the skin temperature can change quite a lot.

When we are worried or anxious our skin becomes cooler. When we are terrified we can break out in a cold sweat. So of course when we are profoundly relaxed the skin is always warm and dry.

Say "Well done, you know that the body temperature stays constant. Now you probably know where the phrases "Chill Out "or "Keep Your Cool" or "Cool It" comes from.

And tell me. I know this is somewhat bizarre.

Whatever the client states answer "that's correct!"

If client says WARMER

If the client say COOLER

Admitting that it is an unusual question

Micro-Analysis of the Magnifying Glass Metaphor

What does the brain tell you has happened to the size and shape of the body?	Something has changed
That's right.	
It does feel	bigger/smaller/wider/ blobbier.
Now you can know what I mean by melted wax.	
	Making allusion to the amnestic loop
So correct me if I'm wrong. But you have just changed your perception of body size, shape, weight and temperature and become incredibly relaxed. True?	
Well that's amazing because I never asked you to change any of these things. I just told you a story of two naughty children playing with a magnifying glass and then I asked you to focus on each part of THE body.	
The word that I used was the word FOCUS. I have no recollection of asking you to become	
	Insert all the changes in body perception in feedback
Would you like to learn how to be able to reproduce this amazing state of relaxation any time that you want in less than sixty seconds?	
Everyone always says "Yes". I think we both know why.	
	Shared knowledge in friendly voice

So let me bring you of out of hypnosis in order to teach you self-hypnosis.

I'm going to simply count from 1 to 10

When I reach the count of 8 THE eyes will open, spontaneously all by THEMSELVES and at 10 you will be fully awake and back to reality.

And if for any reason, you are interested.

You can notice what happens if you TRY to open the eyes BEFORE the count of 8.

1, 2, 3, 4, 5, 6, 7, 8 eyes open 9, 10

3 options happen

1. Opens eyes. " Excellent that proves you are in control. You need to know that."

2. Does not bother. "That's fine. You don't have to try."

3. Eyes cannot open. You probably thought I said you would not be able them, but all I said was notice what happens if you try to open them. Try means fail to the subconscious as I told you already. That's why you are doomed to fail if you listen to the word try.

Now for some Self-Hypnosis.

Micro-Analysis of the Magnifying Glass Metaphor

Take your hands and place them together in a typical 'prayer-like' position.

Then fold the fingers over till the finger tips are touching the knuckles of the other hand.

Then extend the index fingers to as near parallel as possible.

Then simply stare at the gap between the fingers.

Feel the fingers being drawn together by the power of the subconscious.

Drawn together like magnets.

<blockquote>Very occasionally someone might point this physiological fact out. My immediate response if that happens is "Of Course! Magnets between your fingers is just a metaphor - this simple physiological method obviously does not need magnets."

This reply using the word 'obviously' means no further discussion and thus instantly disarms any possible objection.</blockquote>

When the fingers touch just close THE eyes. — dissociative

Take a deep breath in and as you breath out go right back into hypnosis.

Notice how good that feels. — Presupposition of Change

Now just count to ten inside your head and at eight the eyes will open. — Presumption that it was very good

Excellent!

The fingers have to move together because unknown to most people the index and forefingers share a common flexor tendon within the palm of the hand which means that the pressure on the forefinger flexor tendon will almost inevitably bring them together unless they deliberately resist. Focussing on the space causes a degree of dissociation, two areas of the sensory cortex light up when the fingers touch, eyes deliberately close—we go inwards, deep breath in activates the vagus nerve and the slow out breath produces parasympathetic predominance.

Now I want to prove that all hypnosis is self hypnosis so now I want you to repeat what I have just shown you and I will say nothing.

Excellent

Next session, I'll teach you how to get rid of all the unwanted triggers.

Implication of returning for the third session

CHAPTER FIVE

THE SECOND HYPNOSIS SESSION

The Four Fingers Technique

The Four Fingers Technique as described below is a very simple yet rapid hypnosis exercise based on a technique known as hypnotic anchoring. It can also be very useful for a person wishing to access a specific state of mind very rapidly without needing to go through a ritualised hypnotic induction. It is also another generic technique in that it can help very many problems and not just anxiety.

I find it difficult for me to think of any presenting problem where the ability to rapidly displace unwanted emotions, thoughts, physical feelings and images and replace them with desirable emotions, thoughts, physical feelings and images would not be useful. So this again can be used with all of your patients.

It should not be used without significant modification if the patient has certain physical problems e.g. only has one hand, is lacking fingers, has significant finger arthritis or has other disability restricting finger movement.

"Today I want to tell you about something that happened a few years ago."

I was driving with my wife and my three daughters to Taupo.

We were on what is known as the Desert Road.

I happened to glance in the rear-view mirror, and I saw that my youngest daughter in the back seat looked a bit strange.

Her eyes were closed.

Her lips were pursed.

Her fingers were dancing in and out in a vertical line in front of her chest.

It looked weird.

So I said to her, "What are you doing?"

She said, "I'm mentally rehearsing the recorder."

Aah!

The pursed lips the dancing fingers, all now made sense.

I said, "What tune are you playing?"

She said, "My Heart Will Go On, the theme tune from the movie Titanic."

I said. "Oh, I know the one, how does it sound?"

She said, "Fabulous."

She's not short on self-esteem

And I said, "Why don't you play the real recorder?"

She said, "Cause every time you go over a bump, it makes an extra sound."

So I carried on driving and she carried on mentally rehearsing.

A few moments later she suddenly went "Oooh."

I said, "What's up?"

She said, "Oh, my finger slipped and I hit a bum note."

Everyone in the car laughed, ...there had been absolute silence.

But it was one of those moments when I suddenly realised, 'What have I just seen and heard.'

She wasn't repeating the tune in her head from memory because she was taken by surprise by the bum note.

To hear a bum note that surprised her, she must have been taking the information from her fingers to hear the notes in her imagination.

A certain finger position creates the sound of an A, another finger position is a C, and so on.

And when her fingers are not quite covering the correct hole position, she hears a bum note.

A horrible screeching sound.

And I wondered, 'Well how could I apply that to the many people who come with all sorts of problems.'

And as we drove along the Desert Road, my mind was whizzing, and when we got to Turangi I had a brainwave.

I stopped the car and asked my wife to take over the driving.

And all the way along the shore of Lake Taupo I wrote and wrote and wrote, and here's what I came up with.

What I want you to do, is I want you to take your right thumb, and place it against the tip of your right index finger.

That's good!

Now having done that you have activated your left hemisphere in the motor cortex representing those two fingers.

And they're touching.

You can feel they're touching, where they're touching.

And this awareness of touching happens in another nearby area in your left hemisphere that's called the sensory cortex.

Now what I want you to do is, I want you to create a virtual triangle and associate that specific motor and sensory cortex combination with a memory.

I want you to go into your emotional memories and to remember a loving experience, an experience of loving, or of being loved.

It can be recent, or distant, trivial or profound.

When you can remember such a loving experience just nod your head.

O.K.

And now that will be locked into the left front of your brain.

The frontal lobe

Now take the thumb and press it against the next finger.

Now that is a slightly different part of the motor cortex and a slightly different sensory cortex area.

This time I want you to remember the sound of someone paying you a compliment.

Hear the sound of a voice complimenting you.

Saying nice things about you.

And I want you to hear it the way it was meant to be heard.

When you can hear that sound, when you can remember that, just nod your head.

Someone complimenting you.

OK.

And this memory is stored at the side of the brain in the part where we store the memory of sounds.

The parietal lobe.

Now take your thumb and press it against the next finger.

That's good!

Again this is a slightly different motor and sensory area.

This time, I want you to remember a time of what I call honest to goodness tiredness, healthy tiredness.

Say, after a long bush walk?

A heavy day of gardening or chopping up wood?

When you were honest to goodness tired.

And you can feel that in your entire body.

And when you've got a memory of that just nod your head.

That memory is stored in the base of the brain, in what's called the brain stem or cerebellum.

Then take the thumb and press it against the little finger, and this time I want you to remember seeing something, something that was visually beautiful to look at.

And when you can remember seeing something that was visually beautiful, aesthetically pleasing to the eye, just nod your head.

OK.

Now that's stored in the rear of the brain, in the part called the occipital lobe.

You might know that the visual cortex of the brain is in the rear of the brain.

And release the fingers.

Now take the thumb, and press it against the index finger, relive that loving experience.

You only have to do this a few of times to reinforce the message and it becomes set in concrete.

And then take the thumb and press it against the next finger, and you can hear that compliment, when you can hear it just nod your head.

Yeah.

Then take the thumb and press it against the next finger, and you can feel your whole body, experiencing honest to goodness tiredness.

That's right!

And then touch the little finger.

That image of visual beauty comes to mind.

Now release the finger.

Now, these settings and signals aren't set in concrete yet, if you want to change them you are welcome to, to get ones that you are happy with.

Then what you can do is, you can practice them in hypnosis.

Then you can access them out of hypnosis.

Now in my experience, nervousness for something like public speaking has got different aspects to it.

There's a bad feeling, there's a negative internal commentary going on, "Oh my God it's going to be terrible, Oh for goodness look who's here, Oh look at the number of people here".

Then there's a mental tiredness, everything is all screwed up and tense.

And there can be all sorts of unpleasant images of squirming, gabbling away and all sorts of things like that.

So what you're going to learn to do, is to cover the bases, to engage the line.

You can, having done this a few times in hypnosis, out of hypnosis, you can simply put those fingers together and you can have instantly within your brain, in the frontal lobe, a loving experience, then the sound of a compliment, a healthy tiredness, a thing of beauty.

You can literally access these at your fingertips, just as you can access the state of hypnosis, between the two index fingers of each hand.

And you'll find this quite interesting, even simpler than what we did last time.

Does it make sense?

Now each finger has got a top, a middle and a bottom, and if you want, you can load in 3 memories, one for the top, one for the middle, one for the bottom.

You can store 3 loving memories, on that one finger.

3 compliments on the next finger, 3 times of healthy tiredness, 3 things of visual beauty.

You can have 12 accessible memories for all four quadrants of the left-brain hemisphere, literally accessible by touching two fingers.

Now anxiety is always about the future.

We only get anxious about the future.

We do not get anxious about yesterday or last week.

And since we do not know the future and have no memory of the future we create anxiety by imagining the future.

Now imagination lives in the right side of the brain.

And the right hemisphere as you probably know controls the left hand.

Well, with the left hand, you can use the same sort of concept of thumb touching fingers, but it's even better to make it that left index finger equals a <u>future</u> memory of loving.

You have to make it up, it hasn't happened yet, so you use your creativity, your imagination, to imagine a future loving scenario.

Perhaps a romantic holiday next summer.

Then you, touch the next finger, and you hear a compliment that's going to be delivered probably next year, or 10 years from now.

Perhaps when you win some award.

Then you press the next finger and you remember a time of healthy tiredness like when you've just reached the top of that big hill in Hawaii when you go to that fabulous holiday.

Then the time of visual beauty of seeing the sun set over the Caribbean as you cruise on the yacht that you won with your lottery ticket along with the person that you love.

You can make up all these things, when you store them even though they're false, they get stored in the same areas of the brain as false memories, and you can access them.

Now you can store up to 12 memories on each hand, that's 24.

You can play a hell a lot of tunes with 24 notes, you can do the basic 1, 2, 3, 4 or you can do 5, 6, 7, 8.

You can do the 3, 11, 19, and 21.

You can have all sorts of options, you can play them in sequence, or you can predominate with a bit of one or the other.

If you're feeling a bit unloved, do a bit more loving memories, if you're doing a bit of negative commentary, give yourself plenty of positive feedback.

I taught this to one man, and he came back a week later and said, "Doc, but if you take the left hand and press it against the front and back of the right hand and vice versa you can quadruple, you can get 196."

And there's two bits to each thumb, that's an extra 4, that's 200.

It wouldn't surprise you to hear that he had obsessive-compulsive disorder.

It's very simple, you can learn to access various things.

You can choose your thoughts.

Now we can do 5 seconds for each finger, say 4 fingers on one hand, 4 fingers on the other.

That's 8 fingers for 5 seconds.

That will take 40 seconds.

You will access the left front of the brain, the left side of the brain, the left base of the brain, the left rear of the brain.

Then the right front of the brain the right side of the brain the right base of the brain the right rear of the brain.

4 wonderful things of the past, 4 wonderful things of the future, versus one unpleasant thing in the present.

All the unpleasant thoughts that you generate usually comes from those centres.

We are going to engage the line, we are going to have it pre-programmed, a manual over ride, literally manual, 'man' is from Latin 'manus' for 'the hand.'

The Second Hypnosis Session

A manual over ride for any automatic negative thinking, no wonder I was excited, writing away.

By the time I had reached Taupo, I had figured out all the major components of the brain, what did they do, and I realised you could deliberately access them.

I don't know if you've ever learnt to play a musical instrument—have you?

Well if you had this would be obvious to you.

If you've ever seen someone playing a musical instrument, it's amazing, their fingers seem to have a life of their own, they don't have to stop and think, 'now where do I put my fingers for the next note,' they seem to go automatically, all by themselves, it's amazing.

Even though you haven't learnt a musical instrument, this is much easier to learn than the piano or the recorder, because for the recorder, for instance, you have to put your fingers in a certain position to equal a C, for instance.

Learning to play the fingers is so much easier.

My wife and I were on a plane trip to America a while ago, I was sitting by the window seat, she was in the middle, and there was a bloke next to us who had the aisle seat.

His tray top was still down from the meal, and I saw him sort of absentmindedly tapping on the tray top.

My wife gave me one of those nudges, I'm sure you know the kind of nudge that I mean.

"Look at this!"

And I looked at the bloke and he soon stopped.

She said, "That was fabulous!"

He blushed.

I said, "What are you talking about?"

She said, "Didn't you hear it?"

I said, "What?"

She said, "The Moonlight Sonata."

I said, "Pardon?"

She said, "He was playing the Moonlight Sonata, it was wonderful."

He said, "Well I'm going across to Los Angeles to audition for the conservatorium."

She said, "Well, if you play like that you'll get in."

Then I realised that my wife is a good piano player and so is he.

She was hearing music as she watched his fingers.

Not only hearing the music, but realising it was really good.

She could see the way he put his finger on the 'keys', whether it was delicate or firm, she was hearing that sound.

She then said, "Gosh, you're a wonderful piano player."

He said, "Well I've just won a big prize in Wellington."

Now, you always have your fingers with you.

You can have your hands behind your back, in your pockets, at your side, if you want to.

You can just touch the fingers, you can replace any unwanted thoughts, to thoughts of your choice.

And in a sense we all know this.

I bet there are times when you've had an advertising jingle going through your head that you didn't want to hear.

Trying to make it go away by saying 'Go away' doesn't work.

The way to get rid of an advertising jingle is to think of another one.

Overlay it on top of the first one, use the same area of the brain but this time you be in control.

Then the first one goes away.

I hope you can now see how you can apply this to your situation.

Make sure that you've got at least 4 on each hand, 4 from the past, and 4 from the future.

I've become quite sophisticated with my ones.

I've got the palm side as the recent past; the back of the hand is the distant past.

The palm on the other side is the near future, the back of the hand on the left is when I'm a grandparent.

I don't have any grandchildren at the moment, and I might never have them, but I've got a whole scenario about things I'll be complimented on as a fabulous grandfather.

And whenever I want to think about something, I just basically touch a finger and its there.

But for now, just re orientate yourself to the present, count to 10 in your own head, at 8 let your eyes open.

Practice this technique in hypnosis and then use it whenever you want out of hypnosis.

CHAPTER SIX

ANALYSIS OF THE FOUR FINGERS TECHNIQUE

	The opening line is typical storytelling format
Today I want to tell you about something that happened a few years ago.	Once upon a time
I was driving with my wife and my three daughters to Taupo.	Scene setting of a journey to a typical holiday place
I know the road pretty well.	Most New Zealand listeners and most of my patients live in Wellington will automatically think, "So do I."
	The road to Taupo is on the main highway between Wellington, the capital city, and Auckland, the largest city
We had just passed through Waiouru and were on the Desert Road	Even more specific scene setting for locals to visualise
I happened to glance in the rear-view mirror, and I saw that my youngest daughter looked a bit strange	Unusual word, non-specific, requiring some clarification of 'strange'.
She was sat in the middle of the back seat; her eyes were closed. Her lips were pursed.	

Her fingers were dancing in and out in a straight line in front of her chest

Clarification thus provided of 'looked a bit strange'

It looked weird

To enhance the effect of looked strange

Now comes an 'I said', 'She said' segment

So I said to her, "What are you doing?"

She said, "I'm mentally rehearsing the recorder."

Aah! The pursed lips, the dancing fingers, all now made sense
I said, "What are you playing?"

She said, "My Heart Will Go On, the theme tune from Titanic."

I said. "Oh, I know the one, how does it sound?"

She said, "Fabulous."

She's not short on self-esteem

This short, slightly satirical sentence tends to enhance therapist—client rapport. The listener agrees with the speaker that someone who says 'Fabulous' is not short of self-esteem. It also enhances the listener's belief that she is a skilled recorder player

And I said, "Why don't you play the real recorder?"

She carries it with her everywhere.

A passionate musician

She said, "Cause every time you go over a bump, it makes an extra sound."

Fair point!

So I said, "I'll tell you what, you carry on playing it inside your head, and you can play the real one when we get to Taupo."

She said, "Sure, I'll give you a concert". She must be good

I carried on driving and she carried on mentally rehearsing.

A few moments later she suddenly went "Oooh."

I said, "What's up?"

She said, "Oh, my finger slipped and I hit a bum note."

Everyone in the car laughed, 'hit a bum note' ... there had been absolute silence.

But it was one of those moments when I suddenly realised, 'Wait a moment what have I just seen and heard.' Inspirational insight

She wasn't repeating the tune in her head and moving her fingers.

To hear a bum note that surprised her, she must have been taking the information from her fingers to hear the notes.

A certain finger position is an A, another finger position is a C, and so on.

Does this make sense? Clarification of patient understanding

107

And when her fingers are not quite covering the right hole position, she hears a bum note.

A horrible screeching sound.

And I wondered, 'Well how could I apply that to the people who come and sit in the big black chair, with all sorts of problems.'

And as we drove along the Desert Road, my mind was whizzing, and when we got to Turangi,   Locals know that this the next town

I stopped the car and asked my wife to take over the driving.

And all the way along the lakeshore I wrote and wrote and wrote, and here's what I came up with.   Creativity

What I want you to do,   Direct suggestion insert patient name

Is I want you to take your right thumb, and place it against

The tip of THE   Dissociative 'the'

Right index finger.

That's good!   Congratulations

Now   Present

Having done that   Referring to immediate past

You have activated   Much more active than simply 'used'

Your brain.   Truism

Yes Set

Analysis of the Four Fingers Technique

You've activated in your left hemisphere the motor cortex of those two fingers	Y
and you've brought them together	Y
And they're touching	Y
You can feel they're touching	Y
<u>where</u> they're touching	Y
And this awareness of touching happens in an area in your left hemisphere that's called the sensory cortex.	Y
Now what I want you to do is,	
I want you to associate	Helpful suggestion
that motor and sensory cortex combination with a memory.	
I want you to remember a loving experience, an experience of loving, or of being loved.	
It can be recent, or distant, trivial or profound	Bind of comparable options
When	Presupposition
you can remember a loving experience just nod your head.	
O.K.	
And now that will be locked into your mind, just as my daughter locked in the finger position for a C note.	

109

Now the index finger memory, the loving memory, is stored in the front part of the brain, the frontal lobe it's called.

Now take the thumb and press it against the next finger.

Now that is a slightly different part of the motor cortex and a slightly different sensory cortex area.

Truism

This time I want you to remember the sound of someone paying you a compliment.

Hear the sound of a voice complimenting you.

Auditory recall

And I want you to hear it the way it was meant to be heard.

Taking the perspective of the person speaking the compliment

When you can hear that sound, when you can remember that, just nod your head.

This is easy

Someone complimenting you.

OK.

Well done

And this memory is stored at the side of the brain in a place that's called the parietal lobe, in an area called the parietal lobe.

Then you are making a connection between the motor cortex, sensory cortex, and the parietal lobe side of the brain.

Scientific validity

Now take your thumb and press it against the next finger.

That's good!

Praise

Again this is a slightly different motor and sensory area.	
This time, I want you to remember	Age regression
a time of what I call honest to goodness tiredness, healthy tiredness.	Not fatigue or exhaustion
Say, after a long bush walk?	
A heavy day of gardening or chopping up wood?	
When you were tuckered out at the end of the day.	
When you were honest to goodness tired.	Healthy—job well done
And you can feel that in your entire body.	Kinaesthetic suggestion
And when you've got a memory of that just nod your head.	
There you are that was easy.	More praise
That memory is stored in the base of the brain, in what's called the brain stem or cerebellum.	
Then take the thumb and press it against the little finger, and this time I want you to remember seeing something, something that was visually beautiful to look at.	
And when you can remember seeing something that was visually beautiful, aesthetically pleasing to the eye, just nod your head.	
OK.	Well done

Now that's stored in the rear of the brain, in the part called the occipital lobe which is the home of the visual memory cortex.	Scientific validity
You might already know that the visual cortex of the brain is in the rear of the brain.	Or might not
And release the fingers.	
Now take the thumb, and press it against the index finger, relive that loving experience.	Age regression
You only have to do this a few of times to reinforce the message and it becomes set in concrete.	Post hypnotic suggestion of permanence
And then take the thumb and press it against the next finger, and you can hear that compliment, when you can hear it just nod your head.	Presumption
Yeah.	Praise
Then take the thumb and press it against the next finger, and you can feel your whole body, experiencing honest to goodness tiredness.	
That's right!	Praise
And then touch the little finger.	
That image of visual beauty comes to mind.	
Now release the finger.	
Now, these settings and signals aren't set in concrete yet, if you want to change them you are welcome to, to get ones that you are happy with.	

Analysis of the Four Fingers Technique

Then what you can do is, you can practice them in hypnosis.	
Then you can access them out of hypnosis.	Said as a truism
Now in my experience,	May be different for listener
Nervousness	A lesser form of anxiety
For something like public speaking has got different aspects to it.	
There's a bad feeling, there's a negative internal commentary going on, "Oh my God it's going to be terrible, Oh for goodness look who's here, Oh look at the number of people here".	
Then there's a mental tiredness, everything is all screwed up and tense.	
And there can be all sorts of unpleasant images of squirming, gabbling away and all sorts of things like that.	
So what you're going to learn to do,	Presupposition
Is to cover the bases, to engage the line.	Two metaphors
You can, having done this a few times in hypnosis, out of hypnosis, you can simply put those fingers together and you can have instantly within your brain, in the frontal lobe, a loving experience, then the sound of a compliment, a healthy tiredness, a thing of beauty.	

You can literally access these at your fingertips, just as you can access the state of hypnosis, between the two index fingers of each hand.	Truism
And you'll find this quite interesting, even simpler than what we did last time.	Suggestion of interesting and simple
Does it make sense?	Checking that it does
Now each finger has got a top, a middle and a bottom,	Y
And if you want, you can load in 3 memories,	Y
One for the top,	Y
One for the middle,	Y
One for the bottom.	Y
You can store 3 loving memories, on that one finger.	Y
3 compliments on the next finger, 3 times of healthy tiredness, 3 things of visual beauty.	
You can have 12 accessible memories for all four quadrants of the left-brain hemisphere, literally accessible by touching two fingers.	
Now anxiety is always about the future.	
We only get anxious about the future. We do not get anxious about yesterday or last week.	
And since we do not know the future and have no memory of the future we create anxiety by imagining the future.	Truisms

Analysis of the Four Fingers Technique

Now imagination lives in the right side of the brain.

And the right hemisphere as you probably know controls the left hand.

Well, with the left hand, you can use the same sort of concept of thumb touching fingers, but it's even better to make it that the left index finger equals a <u>future</u> memory of loving.

A future memory is a false memory

You have to make it up, it hasn't happened yet, so you use your creativity, your imagination, to imagine a future loving scenario.

A positive false memory of the future

Perhaps a romantic holiday next summer.

Then you, touch the next finger, and you hear a compliment that's going to be delivered probably next year, or 10 years from now.

Perhaps when you win some award.

You will be successful—ego strengthening

Then you press the next finger and you remember a time of healthy tiredness like when you've just reached the top of that big hill in Hawaii when you go to that fabulous holiday.

Kinaesthetic and visual hallucination

Then the time of visual beauty of seeing the sun set over the Caribbean as you cruise on the yacht that you won with your lottery ticket along with the person that you love.

Visualisation

115

You can make up all these things, when you store them even though they're false, they get stored in the same areas of the brain as false memories, and you can access them.   **Presumption**

Now you can store up to 12 memories on each hand, that's 24.

You can play a hell a lot of tunes with 24 notes, you can do the basic 1, 2, 3, 4 or you can do 5, 6, 7, 8.

You can do the 3, 11, 19, and 21.

You can have all sorts of options, you can play them in sequence, or you can predominate with a bit of one or the other.

If you're feeling a bit unloved, do a bit   **Versatility**
more loving memories, if you're doing a bit of negative commentary, give yourself plenty of positive feedback.

I taught this to one man, and he came back a week later and said, "Doc, but if you take the left hand and press it against the front and back of the right hand and vice versa you can quadruple, you can get 196.

And there's two bits to each thumb, that's an extra 4, that's 200.

It wouldn't surprise you to hear that he   **Gentle humour**
had obsessive-compulsive disorder.

It's very simple, you can learn to access various things. You can choose your thoughts.

Now we can do 5 seconds for each
finger, say 4 fingers on one hand,
4 fingers on the other.

That's 8 fingers for 5 seconds.

That will take 40 seconds.   Truism

You will access the left front of the   Said as a truism
brain, the left side of the brain, the left
base of the brain, the left rear of the
brain.

Then the right front of the brain the
right side of the brain the right base of
the brain the right rear of the brain.

4 wonderful things of the past,
4 wonderful things of the future,
versus one unpleasant thing in the
present.

All the unpleasant thoughts that you
generate usually comes from those
centres.

We are going to engage the line, we
are going to have it pre-programmed,
a manual over ride, literally manual,
'man' is from Latin 'manus' for 'the
hand.'

A manual over ride for any automatic
negative thinking, no wonder I was
excited, writing away.

By the time I had reached Taupo, I had   The next few sentences are
figured out all the major components   embellishment of the technique
of the brain, what did they do, and I   by storytelling
realised you could deliberately access
them.

I don't know if you've ever learnt to
play a musical instrument—have you?

Well if you had this would be obvious
to you.

If you've ever seen someone playing a
musical instrument, it's amazing, their
fingers seem to have a life of their own,
they don't have to stop and think, 'now
where do I put my fingers for the next
note,' they seem to go automatically,
all by themselves, it's amazing.

Even though you haven't learnt a
musical instrument, this is much
easier to learn than the piano or the
recorder, because for the recorder, for
instance, you have to put your fingers
in a certain position to equal a C, for
instance.

Learning to play the fingers is so much
easier.

My wife and I were on a plane trip
to America a while ago, I was sitting
by the window seat, she was in the
middle, and there was a bloke next
to us who had the aisle seat.

His tray top was still down from
the meal, and I saw him sort
of absentmindedly tapping on
the tray top.

My wife gave me one of those nudges,
I'm sure you know the kind of nudge
that I mean. "Look at this!"

And I looked at the bloke and he soon stopped.

She said, "That was fabulous!"

He blushed.

I said, "What are you talking about?"

She said, "Didn't you hear it?"

I said, "What?"

She said, "The Moonlight Sonata."

I said, "Pardon?"

She said, "He was playing the Moonlight Sonata, it was wonderful."

He said, "Well I'm going across to Los Angeles to audition for the conservatorium."

She said, "Well, if you play like that you'll get in."

Then I realised that my wife is a good piano player and so is he.

She was hearing music as she watched his fingers. Not only hearing the music, but realising it was really good.

She could see the way he put his finger on the 'keys', whether it was delicate or firm, she was hearing that sound.

She then said, "Gosh, you're a wonderful piano player."

He said, "Well I've just won a big prize in Wellington."

How to Cure Anxiety in Just Five Therapy Sessions

She was right.

It's fascinating.   (It still fascinates me)

Now, you always have your fingers with you.   Truism

You can have your hands behind your back, in your pockets, at your side, if you want to.   Truism

You can just touch the fingers, you can replace any unwanted thoughts, to thoughts of your choice.

And in a sense we all know this.   Common innate knowledge

I bet there are times when you've had an advertising jingle going through your head that you didn't want to hear.

Trying to make it go away by saying 'Go away' doesn't work.

The way to get rid of an advertising jingle is to think of another jingle.

Overlay it on top of the first one, use the same area of the brain but this time you be in control.

Then the first one goes away.

I hope you can now see how you can apply this to your situation.

Make sure that you've got at least 4 on each hand, 4 from the past, and 4 from the future.

I've become quite sophisticated with my ones.   Further extension of the method

I've got the palm side as the recent past; the back of the hand is the distant past.

The palm on the other side is the near future, the back of the hand on the left is when I'm a grandparent.

I don't have any grandchildren at the moment, and I might never have them, but I've got a whole scenario about things I'll be complimented on as a fabulous grandfather.

And whenever I want to think about something, I just basically touch a finger and it's there. | If I can do this then so can you

But for now, just re orientate yourself to the present, count to 10 in your own head, at 8 let your eyes open. | Reorientation

Practice this technique in hypnosis and then use it whenever you want out of hypnosis. | Post hypnotic suggestion

CHAPTER SEVEN

THE SILLY VOICE METAPHOR— THE LIE DETECTOR EXERCISE

As I have stated before—Anxiety is caused by having a mistaken belief and then making the mistake of believing it. The previous chapter explains how to deal with the first part of the problem and this chapter shows how to develop a lie detector. An instant polygraph. It is easy and simple to use and allows us to distinguish thoughts that are unpleasant but true from that that are unpleasant and untrue.

Silly Voice Metaphor

I want you to recall a worry or a thought that bothers you. Hear the sound of your thoughts. I hope that you are hearing your own voice inside your head. If you are hearing the CIA or aliens or God, then we have a vastly different problem.	Gentle Humour
As you listen to the sound of your own inner voice. I'd like you to tell me about the tone of that voice. Give me a few adjectives to describe the tone of that voice that of course, only you can hear.	Allow space for the patient to articulate spontaneously but if they struggle for descriptions of tone then ask if it sounds weak or strong, is it soft or harsh, is it bossy or sad, is it critical or gentle, is it believable?

Now take that same	Harsh, bossy, believable
Thought, the exact same words as before and place them on the	Dissociative
Shoulder. Now I want you change the tone of the voice to a cartoon voice or a squeaky voice of perhaps a little leprechaun talking with a broad Irish accent. The more ridiculous the voice the better.	
How believable does it sound now?	
Now let's humiliate the	Dissociative
Voice even more. Let's have it speaking in the silly voice from the	Dissociative
armpit. The hot, dark and somewhat smelly armpit in of course a muffled silly voice.	
How believable does that comment now sound?	Supposition of change

What you have already learned is that the believability of any thought is due not to the words but to the tone of the voice with which it is broadcast.

I got the idea for this technique by listening to my wife tell me about her experience as a student teacher in Scotland. She was sent to a primary (elementary) school that was reputed to be the roughest and toughest primary school in the city. I struggle not to smile when I say roughest and toughest PRIMARY school.

The teacher to whom she was assigned had a class of rough and tough six-year-olds.

The Silly Voice Metaphor—The Lie Detector Exercise

The teacher said my wife, "I don't know why the College of Education has sent you here to learn about teaching because this class are totally unteachable. These children do not want to learn. Their older brothers and sisters run about the streets in gangs and all that these children want to do is leave school as soon as possible, never get a qualification or a job, get a government benefit, get enough money for alcohol and drugs, have sex, make babies and probably dead by age 40."

My wife replied, "Surely they cannot have written off their lives at age 6!!!!!"

"You'll see!"

They walked into the classroom and the teacher said, "This is Mrs. McCarthy and she will sit at the side and observe."

The teacher then sat behind her desk and placed a briefcase on the desk and put her head down on the desk and	Spoken in a weak and pathetic and pleading voice

Said

"Get your books out, please

Turn to page 22, please

Let's get on with the maths, please?"

From every desk in the class a pre-prepared paper plane was sequentially tossed at her and she picked up the briefcase to try to defend herself from the incoming missiles. A couple of paper darts landed on the desk under the briefcase and struck her and the class all roared with delight with each successful attempt.

The teacher kept turning to my wife and mouthing "I told you that they were unteachable!"

The only maths that the class learned was perhaps a few tips on velocity and trajectory and how to make paper planes that could fly straight.

That afternoon the teacher sat at the side and my wife, a skinny young woman walked out and stood in front of the desk, no briefcase. Unmissable target. The class licked their lips. 'Fresh meat. We will rip her a new one.'

But to their surprise she folded her arms across her chest in a very defiant way and the class all went silent. She then eyeballed the entire class and boy I can tell you that you do not want to be on the receiving end of her eyeball stare. The class all seemed to hold their breath for an eternity. Just when the silence was unbearable, she spoke in a deep and powerful voice.

Do So!

"GET YOUR BOOKS OUT, THANK YOU.

TURN TO PAGE 23, THANK YOU

LET'S GET ON THE WITH MATHS, THANK YOU."

And every child in the class left alone their prepared paper planes and reached for their books and turned to page 23. The only sound was the sound of the teacher's jaw hitting the floor. The lesson went fabulously but she realised that someone would eventually challenge her authority. She guessed that it would be Tommy, the redhead in the front row, who seemed to be the leader of the class gang. Sure enough, after about ten minutes, Tommy looked up at her with a sneer on his face and a look that silently screamed 'Oi, don't you know that I run this class.'

The Silly Voice Metaphor—The Lie Detector Exercise

My wife swiveled around and eyeballed Tommy. Tommy blinked. Fatal mistake. She took two giant and silent steps towards him and when Tommy opened his eyes, expecting her to still be standing at the desk, she was right in his face. Tommy's head went reflexly back and down and there was an audible indrawing of breath from the rest of the class as they collectively inhaled and thought 'even big Tommy is scared of her.'

The lesson went fabulously and when the bell rang at the end of the day the class all filed out and said, "That was great lesson miss. We learned a lot. You're a great teacher miss. Our teacher is shit. Really shit miss. Are you coming back tomorrow?

"I'll be here all week."

"Fantastic, looking forward to it."

As the last child left the room the classroom teacher said, "That was incredible. I can't believe what I've just seen. You had them listening to every word and not a single plane was evened touched let alone thrown. How did you get them to listen to you?"

"Do you really not know?"

"I wish that I did."

"Well, this morning you sounded weak and pathetic and pleading. These children live in the street and the street hates and despises weakness. Weakness is to be stamped on, stomped on and stabbed. The street respects strength and power. Three times you politely said 'please' and this gives the power to the listener to say yeah or nay and three times they all said nay. You brought in a pre-prepared shield which was a non-verbal suggestion of 'throw things at me and I will try to defend myself'.

When I stood in front of the desk with no shield, I was marching into the lion's den. I had no shield and was an unmissable target. I dared them to toss a plane. I then defiantly folded my arms and eyeballed them. They blinked. When I spoke, I sounded like a gang leader. A voice that expected to be obeyed. They have heard voices like that in the street and if you did not obey them instantly then you received a kick up the backside or a whack across the head. I then really messed with their heads. Three times instead of saying please I said thank you. Thank you is the polite phrase after you have done something or agreed to do something. But when it takes the usual place of please in a sentence then the listener hears the thanks and assumes that they must have agreed. After all, why else would I be thanking them."

In fact, the same woman last night said to me "Can I have a cup of tea thank you, and a chocolate biscuit thank you and whilst you are there can you turn on the dishwasher thank you. In fact, in 40 years of marriage I cannot remember her ever saying please.

None of this story actually happened but I do not let truth get in the way of a good story. She is actually very polite and does say Please,

Tone of voice is crucial. Some people believe that dogs understand English. I can assure you that they do not. They understand tone of voice. 'Sit' does not work but 'SIT' does.

We learn the importance of tone of voice at an incredibly young age. My two-year-old daughter held a spoon to her doll's mouth and said to the doll "You WILL eat SOME peas, YOUNG LADY!" She perfectly mimicked what she had heard the previous evening. The authority of WLL, The reasonableness of SOME and the sarcasm of YOUNG LADY.

The Silly Voice Metaphor—The Lie Detector Exercise

Here is a sentence,

I never said he stole her purse. You understand that 7-word sentence surely. But now listen again carefully.

I never said he stole her purse. That means someone else did.

I **never** said he stole her purse. That means a complete denial.

I never **said** he stole her purse. That means I hinted at it.

I never said **he** stole her purse. That means someone else did.

I never said he **stole** her purse. That means he borrowed it.

I never said he stole **her** purse. That means it was someone else's purse.

I never said he stole her **purse**. That means he stole her money.

But if I send that as text or an email then what message do I mean? How many times have people taken the wrong meaning from a text or email?

You know how important tone of voice is when speaking but I hope you can now realise that the tone of the nonsense that you think is what MAKES YOU BELIEVE IT. So, if you ever want to have a lie detector at the ready just repeat any thought in a silly voice from your armpit and if it is less believable then you will intuitively know that it is a lie.

Post Hypnotic suggestion at the end of this session

"We communicate a lot of information by our tone of voice. You have always known how to vocally communicate anger, frustration, sadness, worry or joy and so much more. But what about the tone of voice of our thoughts. That also can be broadcast in a bossy, critical, fearful, helpless, negative and believable way and that's why we believe our thoughts. For instance you might know that some people with depression wake each morning and as they open their eyes their first thought is

And here I start speaking in an exaggerated lugubrious sad sack voice

'Not another day like always, oh well I need to get up'. They slowly crawl out of bed and slowly walk to the shower, as if they wear wearing a lead overcoat and pathetically stand in the shower and let the water trickle and wet them. They slowly dab themselves dry and slowly, very slowly, choose some drab coloured clothes and by the time they have left home their day is doomed to be yet another miserable day. I tell them that there's another and better option. From the moment they wake till the time that they leave the front door I want them to think a special song lyric over and over again with defiance and determination. "I get knocked down, but I get up again. Nothings's ever gonna keep me down. I get knocked down, but I get up again. Nothings's ever gonna keep me down" Imagine how they now leap out of bed, stride quickly to the shower, scrub vigorously, dry with energy and decide to choose bright colourful clothes. Our life is what our thoughts make it. Let this be your regular morning thought."

CHAPTER EIGHT

HOW TO THINK LIKE AN OPTIMIST. THE 3 P'S

The next step in the treatment of anxiety is teaching the patient how to edit their thinking from a pessimistic style to an optimistic style. This next session explains the concept of attributional style using a variety of examples or vignettes that they can easily visualise. Again, it is a generic technique that is useful for many pessimistic patients presenting with a variety of problems.

Given that there are entire books written about attributional style I cannot fully explain attributional style in detail but my aim is to have people realise that their explanation of life events does not have to be the only possible explanation. I point out the book where they can learn more. It's called The Optimistic Child and written by Martin Seligman. If they buy and read this book aloud then they do not need this next session. As a species we have been learning from reading for only a few hundred years but we have been listening for learning for thousands of years. That is the crucial importance of reading aloud. I have often had 3 children and 2 adults each reading aloud two pages of the book after dinner each night. That's 10 pages of information absorbed aurally by 5 people each evening. It helps bonds the family as a unit on a shared and equal task and allows informed discussion after the session. It also helps young people, in particular, feel confident about reading aloud. They have to realise as a family that their current attributional style is worsening their problem.

Most patients that we meet have a core of pessimism that underlies their problem. Optimists seldom present for therapy as they tend to assume that their problems will soon pass. I often tell people that they might be Successful Pessimists. A Successful Pessimist has a core of pessimism that they learned in childhood but a thin veneer of Optimism that they project to the world. This veneer comes off if they perceive that they have somehow lost control and the core of pessimism learned in childhood erupts and starts the cascade towards anxiety.

I choose to deliver this particular hypnosis session in a long form story telling way. By now you will have realised that each word is carefully chosen and if you are interested you may wish to analyse the micro structure of the session. You will now probably be able to notice the deliberate suggestions and the presumptions and truisms and so on more easily as you read along.

"So just sit back and put yourself into hypnosis.

Take as much time as you like.

Just close your eyes and listen to the sound of my voice.

Today you are going to learn how to be able to be far more optimistic.

What you will learn in this session is based on the work of Professor Martin Seligman from America who has written a fascinating book called Learned Optimism and a more readable one called The Optimistic Child which I would encourage you obtain a copy of and to read it aloud so that you hear it which helps memory.

In the book he describes what he calls our attributional style.

It turns out that we all have what he calls an 'attributional style'.

What this means is that we have a style of attributing a reason, a meaning or an explanation to the various events that happen in our life.

We do this whether the events are good or whether they are bad.

It turns out that optimists and pessimists have a hugely different attributional style.

Children ask lots of questions that start with WHY.

As adults we do the same.

Why has this happened?

Why do I feel this way?

For most Why questions there can often be three categories of answer.

Seligman calls them the 3P's

The first P is Personal. As in "It's my fault."

The opposite of Personal is Impersonal.

That reaction elicits the belief that "It's someone else's fault."

The next P is Permanent.

As in "It always happens."

Its opposite is of course Temporary.

"It sometimes happens."

The third P is Pervasive or widespread. As in "It affects absolutely everything"

The opposite of Pervasive is Specific. As in "It only affects this one thing."

Let me explain how this attributional style works.

Let's take the example of two employees at work.

One is an extreme pessimist and the other is an extreme optimist.

You probably won't be like either of these two types given they are extreme examples but see which ones thinking style you are most similar to.

I suspect that you can already guess which one it will be.

Let's say that that the boss hands the pessimist a note and it reads "You're sacked. You're fired. You're dismissed. Get out of here."

The Pessimist mentally instantly reacts with a Personal explanation.

"What did I do wrong?

What did I stuff up?

What mistake did I make to be fired?"

The Optimist who is given the same note on the other hand reacts with an Impersonal explanation.

"Gee the firm must be in trouble.

It must be due to the high exchange rate, or perhaps,

I knew that boss hated me."

They never assume that the sacking had anything to do with them. They are quick to blame someone or something else.

The Pessimist then comes out with some Permanent thinking, "I might never get another job.

I might never get a job as good as this one.

I might have to leave town to get a job. I might have to go to another country to get a job."

The Optimist thoughts however are that the problem is just temporary "I've had 5 jobs already.

I'm sure I'll be able to find a new one soon.

I might even take the redundancy money and head to Brisbane in Australia.

I hear that there are some great jobs there and lots more sunshine. This could turn out to be a blessing in disguise."

The Pessimist thoughts become pervasive and they think. "I'm a failure.

I'm a loser.

I've lost my job.

I'm a loser, a failure, a huge disappointment to my parents.

I'm a loser to my partner.

I'm a loser to my children.

I'm a loser to my sports team.

I'm a complete loser."

The Optimist on the other hand immediately thinks along the following far more specific lines.

"Oh well. I lost this job but not to worry I'll soon get another one.

I still get on well with my parents and still get on well with my partner and with my children and I still get on well with my sports team.

It's only a minor setback.

Everything else in my life is good."

They thus make their problem quite specific.

On the other hand when good things happen then the whole style of thinking turns around 180 degrees.

Let's take the scenario with the extreme optimist and the extreme pessimist again.

This time the boss hands over a note and the pessimist reads it and reads "Here is a bonus cheque." and beside the note is a cheque for $3000 dollars.

This remember comes completely out of the blue.

The Pessimist's reaction now is Impersonal.

A typical pessimistic reaction might be.

"A bonus cheque.

The firm must have had a record profit.

My department must have won that big contract.

And if the pessimist is a gorgeous woman she might be thinking.

Why has the boss singled me out for a bonus cheque?

What is their ulterior motive?

Why are they giving me this?"

The optimist on the other hand has a completely different reaction. The first thoughts of an optimist would perhaps be on the lines of "Of course I've been given a bonus.

I'm the best worker here.

I'm superb at the job.

I'm the best salesperson that they have ever had."

I ask you to ponder for a moment and consider how many people you have heard talking like that in your country.

Very few if any people in New Zealand ever talk like that I can tell you.

In terms of permanency the pessimist thinks in terms of "A 3000-dollar bonus at this time of year.

That's really strange.

We normally only ever get a bonus at Christmas time.

We never get two bonuses in the same year.

That's never happened before.

So what does that mean?

Does that mean that everyone else will be getting their bonus at Christmas and I won't be?

That's when I could really use a bonus.

But wait, does that mean that they will probably lay me off before Christmas.

That's the only explanation. It's not really a bonus cheque it's a redundancy cheque."

The Optimist however is completely different.

Their thinking becomes along permanent lines.

They think "Wow 3000 dollars for being the best worker.

Imagine what the Christmas bonus will be like.

And in the New Year they are doing a promotion round.

I'll be first in the queue for promotion.

This year is going to be a great one and next year is going to be even better."

In terms of pervasiveness the pessimistic thinks along the lines of "Well I've got a bonus cheque in my pocket but my car still rattles and that always annoys me.

$3000 won't buy me a new car.

$3000 won't even buy me a new engine.

And I'm travelling home to a relationship that's second class and on the rocks.

John Lennon was absolutely right—Money can't buy me love.

So what will I have when the money is all gone?

Still with a second-class car and a second-class relationship.

Big deal.

It's only money and it will soon all be gone."

The Optimist on the other hand, particularly if it is man is quite different.

He phones up his wife and says "We are in the money."

I am going to take you out to that fancy Italian restaurant that was reviewed in the paper last night.

We are going to have a slap-up celebration meal.

We are going to have champagne.

The good stuff.

We are going to have a great time'

The odds are he is also thinking "We are going to.....have a cuddle.....shall I say.....or perhaps something else......all night long."

All the research shows however that the most realistic people are in fact the mild Pessimists.

They are the most accurate.

The mild and moderate optimists are the most successful, however. They are often the healthier and the wealthier as they take a few risks and obtain the rewards.

The moderate and severe pessimists however are the one who are at most risk of developing anxiety, panic and depression.

The extreme optimists are however incredibly unrealistic.

Take that last example for instance.

The extreme optimist's anticipation usually turns out to be completely wrong.

The Italian restaurant will be fully booked, they will go somewhere else and the steak will be overcooked and he will drink far too much wine and he will simply snooze and snore instead of…..cuddling.

The optimist on waking from this failure however immediately puts the failure behind and thinks.

Right I've still got money left over.

I'll phone the Italian restaurant and get a good table for tonight.

I'll lay off on the booze and then I'll be cuddling all night long.

My particular interest in this is in its application to a common condition known as post-natal depression.

Post-natal depression comes on after the birth of a baby and affects about 10% or 1 in 10 mothers in New Zealand.

Similar figures are common in the rest of the world.

I used to go and visit women who had recently had a baby in my role as a family doctor.

I wondered who would be at risk of developing post-natal depression.

I decided to test for pessimistic thinking.

I waited till the baby cried and I then tossed in a simple yet very revealing WHY question.

I simply asked the mother, "Why does your baby cry so much?"

If she replied. "Because I'm a bad mother "or "I don't know how to look after babies" I would reply Babies cry because they are hungry or thirsty or need to be picked up or some other good reason.

This has got nothing to do with your skills as a mother."

She then might reply "But my baby is always crying.

Day and night.

Perhaps it has colic?

Always? I'd reply.

Your baby was quiet when I came in.

It has only started crying now.

So pick it up, feed it, change it and clothe it.

When the baby stops crying you can put it back in the cot.

Remember that crying is always temporary.

It stops.

She then might reply "But look at the state of the house.

It's filthy and I haven't even made any supper for my husband.

I'm a terrible wife and a mother.

I would say, "Well-you have a sick baby to care for.

That has taken up all of your time today.

Phone up your husband and ask him to bring in some fish and chips on the way home.

Remember sick baby equals takeaway meals for the rest of the family."

I taught this to 900 women and amazingly not a single woman developed post-natal depression.

I explained this result to a visiting American psychologist who was a guest speaker at a local conference that I was attending.

He was impressed and told me that I should present my findings to the Brief Therapy Conference.

I laughed when he said that for the Brief Therapy conference is a bit like the Olympics of Psychology.

It is held every 4 years and always in America.

Approximately 2000 people turn up to the conference and about 700 people apply to be a speaker.

A panel of judges apparently choose the top 24 speaking proposals.

Only 3.5% are chosen.

You can imagine my surprise when I later received a letter from the organisers saying that I had been chosen as one of the speakers.

I then sat down to write the actual speech and not just the proposal.

And I promptly got writer's block.

I kept hitting backspace and delete.

It simply wasn't academic enough.

It wasn't entertaining enough.

It just wasn't good enough.

My wife came into the room.

How are you getting on with the speech she asked?

I told her that I had not even written a title for the speech.

How I kept deleting what I'd written.

She said "You've been doing that for an hour.

I thought that might happen. Here are some gardening clippers.

You can cut the hedge and think about your speech at the same time."

I'm married to this intensely practical Scottish schoolteacher.

I want out and started clipping the hedge and thinking about my speech at the same time.

My neighbour came out to peg up her washing.

She is a young woman with two small children.

She had post-natal depression after each of them.

She was not a patient of mine just a neighbour.

As good neighbours do we chatted across the hedge.

I have never seen anyone peg up washing that quickly before.

Her fingers were a blur of knickers and nappies.

She dropped two pegs. No wonder going at rocket speed.

She picked the pegs off the floor and let out a deep sigh and explained plaintively."

"I'm always dropping things."

She then scurried back into the house.

Those four words hit me like a ton of bricks.

Her unvoiced WHY question was "Why are the pegs on the floor?"

Her reply was I'm, which is personal.

Always, which is permanent and dropping things not just pegs which is pervasiveness.

That's when it dawned on me that if an optimist had dropped a couple of pegs then according to Seligman the optimist would have something along the lines of "These cheap plastic pegs from the Warehouse sometimes slip.

The optimist would have blamed not herself, but the pegs, for being slippery.

The optimist would have said 'sometimes.

The optimist would have believed that it was 'just the cheap plastic pegs that fell'.

Not the more expensive wooden ones.

I wondered why she had rushed back into the house.

Perhaps she had left some muffins in the oven.

Say she goes back in and the muffins are a bit crispy on top.

The pessimist will think.

Typical.

Ruined again.

I can never bake anything.

No wonder my husband calls me the culinary thrombosis of Karori.

That's the clot in the kitchen by the way.

The optimist on the other hand sees the crispy top muffins and thinks. "Oh that's a surprise.

The oven must have been a bit hot today.

But no worries. I'll chop the crispy top off the muffins and stick a bit of cream and jam on them.

I'll call then Mount Ruapehu smoky volcanic muffins.

They'll be extremely popular.

And if a bit of jam runs down the side.

She doesn't write that one off.

She thinks "That's a lahar.

That's unusual.

We can charge more for that one."

If the muffins turn out well the pessimist thinks "Wow that's lucky, just saved them in time before they were ruined.

"Whereas the optimist would think. "Of course they turned out well.

I'm great in the kitchen.

I'm great everywhere."

I raced back into the house and started furiously writing about pegs and muffins.

3 months later I was over in New York at the Brief Therapy Conference.

It was Wednesday breakfast on the morning of my speech.

My plate of bacon and eggs was cooling and congealing on my plate.

My heart rate was over 100.

I was nervous.

At 11 am I would have to address 2,000 people.

Suddenly the woman at the table next to me leaned over and said "Are you that doctor from New Zealand who is talking about how to prevent post-natal depression.

In my best attempt at a Kiwi accent I said "Yes, I am."

My obvious Scottish accent surprised her!

She then said 'We've driven up from Alabama and I'm particularly interested in your presentation later this morning.

I've had post-natal depression with my previous two children and baby number three is on the way.

It says here in the programme that you can learn how to change your style of thinking so that you don't develop anxiety or panic or depression ever again.

Well that just sounds too good to be true."

Ah! Too good to be true.

That a very typical pessimistic Scottish statement.

You have to imagine a wee Scottish minister reaching out for a small glass containing brown liquid that he hopes will be malt whisky and takes a sip of....cold tea.

Ach it was too good to be true.

As if somehow goodness and truth were incompatible.

I heard that dour expression many a time in my younger days.

The woman then reached for a piece of toast and she knocked her cup of black coffee all over the white Damask linen tablecloth.

She leapt to her feet and cried out "Oh I'm such a klutz. I'm always doing things like that."

I hope you recognised her pessimistic style.

I'm personal, always is permanent and things like that is pervasive.

Five minutes later another woman knocked over her coffee cup and exclaimed.

Oh damn these silly cups.

Oh well.

Accidents happen.

Waiter give us another table.

She excused herself and went to the washroom to clean the coffee splash off her skirt.

I spoke to her husband and said, "Your wife is an optimist."

He nodded and said yes.

He told me that she reckons nothing ever gets her down.

She never became anxious or upset.

He reckoned it was because she was a Southern Baptist.

She has great faith he said.

I replied well I reckon she is an incredibly optimistic Southern Baptist.

She is he said.

But how do you know that?

You haven't met her, have you?

No not at all.

But I heard what she said when she knocked over the coffee cup and that was enough to tell me that she was a supreme optimist.

He replied you could tell that from what she said when she spilled the coffee?

Yup

Wow!

You must be that doctor from New Zealand who is speaking at 11 on the conference programme about how to stop being anxious, panicky or depressed.

I thought that was a huge claim.

It certainly sounded too good to be true.

But now I think it might be true.

We will definitely be at your talk.

When I delivered the talk the audience were mostly incredibly quiet and I wondered how my speech was going down.

When I finished, I was astonished to see the entire audience rise to their feet and give me a standing ovation.

Being mostly Americans they were hooting and hollering and yelling and foot stomping.

But none of them could see me any more.

For I had dipped down behind the lectern and was blushing furiously.

I was thinking, "Wow you Americans are so over the top."

You are probably only cheering like that because I'm the only non-American on the programme and you are being polite to a foreigner who has travelled further than anyone else to the conference.

Tone it down guys.

Too much.

You are very generous with your praise."

The chairman was leaping about like a mad thing.

"Wow" he said.

"No wonder you Kiwis have that great Rugby team and that great Yachting team and that great Soccer team."

I thought "Steady on. 2 out of three yes but not our Soccer team."

The chairman said, "You must take some questions."

Suddenly I saw in the front row a man sitting whilst everyone else was standing.

His arms were folded across his chest and there was a look of disappointment or anger or perhaps it was both on his face.

I looked closely at him and I thought that I might have recognised him.

I said to the chairman, "You take the questions.

I will be back in one minute."

I went down to the front row and said, "Are you who I think you are?

He solemnly nodded.

"Ulp!! You look annoyed."

"I'm furious", he said.

"Why?"

He said "Well when I saw in the programme what you were going to talk about, I was really excited but in the very first minute of your speech.

The very first minute.

The batteries of my hearing aid died.

I could not hear a thing.

I knew that if I walked out from the front row to get some batteries then people would think that I was being derogatory, walking out on you.

I couldn't do that.

You are the speaker who has travelled the furthest to be here.

I didn't have my cell phone to phone someone and ask them to bring some batteries.

I tried to lip read but I couldn't.

I'll be honest. For the last twenty minutes I've been secretly hoping that it was a bad speech so that I hadn't missed anything important.

But I have never seen a reception like this for any speaker at this conference ever.

Especially for someone who is not an American.

The reason that I am so annoyed is that as soon as you answer all the questions then people will be asking me what I thought of the speech.

I am the only person in the room who never heard it.

That's why I'm so annoyed."

"I've got a copy of the speech in my bag if you would like to read it."

"I'd love to read it.

Get the chairman to send it down to me but go and take the first question.

The Chairman is calling for you."

As I took the first question that's precisely when it dawned on me that I was a Pessimist.

For if I were an Optimist then I would have taken a few strides forward and taken a deep bow.

I'd probably have thought "Wow, I was great, you guys are lucky to have heard me. I was brilliant."

Instead, as I said earlier, I was hiding behind the podium blushing furiously.

As a pessimist I was thinking the audience was generous rather than that I was good.

An optimist would have assumed that the person sitting down was probably a bit deaf or could not understand a Scottish accent.

I was thinking that I must have annoyed the person by talking about trivial things like muffins and pegs.

Later, when I spoke with him after he had read my speech, he was happy to read that the attributional style could also apply to such trivial things as muffins and pegs.

Apparently, we learn our attributional style before the age of five.

I learned my pessimistic style by listening to both my parents but especially to my father.

I remember when I was twelve that I sat the Scottish Maths examination.

Everyone in the country sat it.

I scored 99%.

Most of my class struggled to score over 60%.

I went home and said to my father that I had scored 99%.

He looked at me and said, "Just the one wrong. Better luck next time."

He instantly focused on the one that I had got wrong rather than on the 99 that I had got right.

He told me that I needed better luck, as if the 99% was due to luck.

Luck is impersonal.

To this very day I have no idea how to have better luck.

Brains, hard work or effort I could do.

But how could I possibly arrange better luck.

'Next time' he had said.

There would not be a next time.

I would never have a chance to repeat the test.

I would always, that is permanently, have failed to reach perfection by one.

I have a confession to make.

A few years ago my own daughter came home from school and proudly stated that she had scored 99% for her French vocabulary test.

I still blush when I recall what my response was.

"Just the one wrong."

"Oops, let me start again.

Fantastic score, excellent result, wonderful student, you will do well, get your two sisters and mother and lets all go out to celebrate a great student and scholar at the 4th P which is Pizza Hutt and I will teach you all about the 3 P's, which is not a pizza topping.

So I taught my daughters what I have taught you.

Then I made a mistake.

I offered my daughters a chance to make some money.

They are the children of Scottish parents and their ears pricked up.

"For the next three months, if I say something pessimistic and you can point this out to me and give me the optimistic translation then I will explain the optimistic give you a dollar."

They said, "Every time you say something pessimistic then we get a dollar?"

"Absolutely.

Now I need to write a cheque for the meal.

Where did I put that bloody pen?"

One of my daughters piped up "That will be a dollar thank you."

"Why?

Was it my use of the word bloody?

Bloody is a bit rude, it has to be a statement that was pessimistic."

"It was, but it wasn't the word bloody that made it so."

"It wasn't?

Well to get the dollar you still have to explain the optimistic translation."

"O.K. You said. 'Where did I put that bloody pen?'

You mislaid it.
Personal.
Your fault.
Pessimistic.

An optimist would have said 'Where did that bloody pen get to?'

The assumption being that the naughty pen had somehow mischievously hidden itself somewhere in your jacket.

Thus impersonal and thus optimistic.

"You have just earned yourself a dollar."

I took a dollar out of my pocket and dropped it on the floor.

"Oops, I dropped it."

She replied, "Well that's two dollars then!"

"How? I did drop it, that a fact. It's surely not pessimistic. It's on the ground, that's the fact."

"The question however is how it got there.

'I dropped it' is a personal clumsiness explanation.

'It slipped' is an impersonal bad luck explanation."

"O.K. you've earned $2."

Over the next three months my daughters earned over $800.

They realized that when I was tired, they could bombard me with WHY questions and I would inevitably eventually reply with an always or perhaps a never which would invariably cost me another dollar.

e.g. 'I decided to come home via Aro Valley. Late again. I'm always making that mistake.'

Now this is taking attributional style down to a micro linguistic level where it is indeed most common.

It cost me $800 over three months to learn how to edit my speech to an optimistic style.

You can get hold of the excellent book by Martin Seligman called Learned Optimism which I heartily endorse or the Optimistic Child which is, I believe, even better for parents to read to their children and will be a lot cheaper way to learn how to think like an Optimist.

The healthy zone for life is between mild pessimism and moderate optimism.

When there is definite risk to you then choose to be mildly pessimistic such as when crossing a road, but when there is no risk to you such as when applying for a job then go to the interview with an optimistic mindset.

This pessimistic to optimistic skill is not an easy skill to master but I believe that it is the most important one to do so.

Translation from what I call Pessimese to Optimese is easier than learning a foreign language because you do not have to learn any other vocabulary as you would with another language.

This translation uses the same vocabulary.

You simply need to learn how to consistently apply the 3P grammar rule.

It takes practice to become bilingual but it is certainly worth learning.

So now you have reached the end of your cure of anxiety.

Anxiety starts with the perception of being out of control and that sparks off your learned Pessimism.

The Pessimism sparks off unwanted emotions, thoughts, physical feelings and images.

These in turn switch on the sympathetic nerves and give you all the symptoms of anxiety.

But now you have learned how to produce a relaxation attack in less than sixty seconds.

You have also learned how to displace and replace unwanted emotions, thoughts, feelings and images with positive versions in less than one second and you have now learned how to think like an optimist.

You thus no longer have to believe that you are out of control as you now have three skills that you never had before and if you can master these three skills by listening and learning these skills then you can lead a happy and optimistic life.

Welcome to the world of happiness.

Now just count to ten in your head and open your eyes to the wonderful future that can be yours."

CHAPTER NINE

THE SPECIAL PLACE OF BLISS

Sometimes when the sessions of therapy were finished a few patients, about 20%, have told me that although they certainly and undeniably felt significantly better they still felt that there was still a problem with some possible residual anxiety.

They fully accepted that they would have to practice the techniques more in order to ingrain them and that they are glad that they have a recording of each session in order to practice perfectly but a few said that they still felt uneasy and so wanted a follow up session to feel completely be cured of their anxiety.

One more session only would have to suffice to achieve this as they were often reaching the limit of their available budget for therapy.

This caused me to doubt that the basic three step process of rapid parasympathetic predominance, etfi displacement and replacement, the silly voice metaphor and learning to think like an optimist was all that was required for all people with anxiety despite the apparent impeccable logic of the method. What was the flaw in my logic?

Something else was obviously required for these few patients.

Something was missing. Something I had not considered. What could it be?

Perhaps the few patients who were not completely cured had something in their personal history that was truly relevant and still present and preventing their complete cure and had not been disclosed. As I explained earlier, I choose not to ask for their historical details. So I then asked these patients, who were not completely cured, to tell me more about their history and to my surprise ALL of them mentioned that as well as having anxiety they also admitted to having significant levels of what they called 'emotional baggage'. Significant psychological damage in their past. Often repeated and long-lasting traumas.

This issue of having significant emotional baggage appeared to be the common theme in those few patients not yet completely cured. This was a large part of 'their unique wrapping paper' to use my previous box of chocolates metaphor.

The reason that it had not occurred to me was that I have no obvious emotional baggage. I am incredibly lucky to have had a wonderful life. I was brought up in a 2 bedroomed house and always knew that I was unconditionally loved and supported by my parents. I was never beaten or abused. I am the eldest of ten children and I never perceived the house as being overcrowded yet of course it was. I never felt a victim and never a second-class citizen despite growing up in a city that deemed that the minority religious group that I belonged to was supposedly inferior. I struggle to think of any significant and persisting trauma in my own life. Sure I have had setbacks and tears. Disappointments and failures of course, yet the key word is 'persisting'—I regard them as just technicalities.

I'm quite a stubborn person and I hate failing. I refuse to accept defeat and so I pledged to find a way to help these people complete the cure of their anxiety.

I therefore had to invent a method that would help people deal with and break free from all of their emotional baggage. I resolved that whatever method I would devise would have to somehow not stir up their past problems or make them relive trauma and that it would also have to be completely confidential and without them ever having to disclose any of their unrelieved issues. They would also not need to solve or even explain their problems to me. Could their 'Wrapping paper be scrunched up and tossed aside? And yet of course all of this would all have to be achieved in a 30–40-minute session.

I therefore over a few weeks invented a technique that could achieve all the above essentials, that I simply call The Special Place of Bliss.

Special Place of Bliss Imagery

There are several previously published versions of "A Special Place" hypnosis scripts. Each has minor variations on the general theme of creating such a place for someone to use when in trance such as being at a beach or perhaps in a lovely garden. Being relaxed and comfortable and feeling secure is a common therapeutic goal of hypnotists. This hypnotic feel good experience temporarily feels good but seldom lasts long.

Beginners to hypnosis often use these prepared scripts, as they are helpful and easy for a novice to read to a patient rather than run out of ideas and come to an embarrassing and sudden stop with no idea about what to say next. These scripts generally contain incredibly positive and helpful ego-strengthening suggestions. Most of these 'Special Place' scripts aim to be soothing and comforting so that they effectively provide a place of emotional rest, safety and tranquillity.

I however wanted much more than that.

The following script, that I simply call the Special Place of Bliss metaphor (SPB) is structurally and contextually non-specific to any problem.

Because of the non-specificity you will find that this script often works well not just with anxiety but with a surprisingly wide range of presenting problems. It can in fact I believe be used as a hypnosis treatment session for virtually all presenting complaints. A therapy graduation session. A final session for every patient to wrap up any and all loose ends.

This powerful exercise can also address and powerfully deal with and resolve many other problems, sometimes even much more significant than the presenting problem, that may not even have been articulated or identified by the patient.

The SPB script as seen below is designed to go far beyond the conventional use of a simple 'special place' script and has additional potential psychotherapeutic benefits beyond just being a simple place of safety and relaxation. It has multiple psychological safety features to prevent abreaction. These are all described in the micro-analysis that follows. These collectively are so effective that I have never encountered any difficult abreaction despite using this technique with many thousands of people.

The premise that underlies this exercise is that it enables each listener to put all of their unique worries and problems (emotional baggage) off to one side and experience a genuine 'state of bliss'.

The basic wording and structure of the script is given below and some of the key hypnotic elements are highlighted in the subsequent chapter.

The Special Place of Bliss

Induction of trance. Usually using 2 finger attraction method as mentioned above.

Deepening of the trance, (using any method you desire)

"Today I'd like to teach you how to experience your very own unique special place of bliss……..

I'd like you to imagine a corridor.

As you walk along the corridor there are doors leading off to the left and to the right.

And at the end of the corridor see a door.

A very inviting sort of door.

You can decide for yourself the size and shape of the door.

Tell me, what colour is the door?

Is the door a plain door or does it have panels?

Does the door have a handle?

Is the handle on the left or on the right?

What colour and shape is the handle?

Now look very closely, does the door seem to open inwards or outwards?

You may be wondering about this door?

About what lies behind the door?

In a few minutes you will discover that behind the door is a special place.

Your very own special place.

A place that your imagination is already creating for you.

It is a special place.

A place of bliss.

Absolute bliss!

Now bliss is an old-fashioned word.

It's not used much nowadays.

Let me be quite clear about what I mean by bliss.

Bliss is a state of mind.

Bliss is far more than just the absence of negativities.

The absence of worries, the absence of problems, concerns, difficulties, traumas and upsets.

Bliss is more than that.

As well as the absence of negativities, bliss is also the positive presence of such concepts as freedom, peace, comfort, joy, happiness, relaxation and rest.

Absolute pleasure.... sheer.....bliss.

So, in order to experience a sense of bliss then we have to, at least on a temporary basis, be able to put all of our problems and worries and concerns off to one side.

So, on your back you will find a backpack.

Take the backpack off and place it in front of you.

Open the backpack.

Inside you will find a collection of stones.

Special stones.

Notice how the stones are somewhat flat, but rounded and smooth, rather like the sort of stones you might find on the bed of a river or a rocky beach perhaps.........

Do you see the special stones?

These stones are special because in hypnosis they are very symbolic.

The stones represent <u>each</u> of your problems.

<u>Every</u> problem.

<u>Every</u> concern.

And because these stones represent <u>every</u> problem, not just the ones that you have told me about.

I want to make one thing clear.

This next part of the exercise will be carried out in <u>total and absolute</u> privacy.

Now by total and absolute privacy I don't just simply mean the normal confidentiality that you would expect and will of course receive from a doctor.

No, I mean far more than that.

By total and absolute privacy I mean that you will do the next part of the exercise entirely inside your own head, in silence.

So that only you will ever know what issues these stones represent for you.

Let me be absolutely clear.

I will never, ever, ask you to talk about the meaning of your stones.

Only you will ever know how many stones are in the backpack.

Again I will never, ever ask you to talk about the number of stones.

And perhaps most importantly of all only you will ever know the weight of each stone.

Obviously, the weight of the stones relates to the weight of the problems.

Again I will never, ever ask you to talk about the weight of any of the stones.

Is that guarantee of privacy completely understood?

These stones represent all of the problems that you have in your mind.

There are the problems of now, the present.

The issues and concerns that are on your mind now, today, this very day.

But there are also stones about the past.

And the past includes yesterday, last week, last month, last year, ten years ago, many years ago.

All the way back to your earliest memories of problems from childhood.

And there can also be stones from the future.

How can this be since the future hasn't happened yet?

Well, these are what I call the "What if?" stones.

Some people carry around stones that represent worries about what might happen in the future.

What could go wrong!

What might not change!

Sometimes these stones are possibilities.

Sometimes remote possibilities.

But some people carry them around like rocks of probabilities.

Or even as huge boulders of certainties.

Your imagination will tell you what size each stone and issue is.

Now look at the stones in the backpack.

This is what I want you to do.

In a few moments I will give you the signal to start emptying the backpack.

This is how I want you to safely empty it.

In a moment I want to you look at the top stone.

It will probably have a label on it.

To let you know what problem it represents.

I want you to read the label and identify the problem.

Then, briefly, pick up the stone and feel the weight of the stone and then place it down on the floor beside the door.

Then turn to the backpack and identify the next stone, feel the weight of that stone and then put it down beside the door.

Keep doing this till the backpack is completely empty.

Then when you have taken the time you need to completely empty your backpack you can let me know that it is empty by raising your right thumb in the air.

Are those instructions clear?

Then turn to the backpack and now start unloading all your problems ....

stone by stone ....
issue by issue ....
problem by problem ....
till the bag is completely empty.
Take all the time you need.
<u>Give the person time to empty their stones. A few useful interjections every so often can be helpful</u>

e.g. Some of the stones are the ones you expected to find there.

Others might be a bit of a surprise.

Some of the stones may be heavier than you had expected.

Some may be surprisingly light.

Some of the stones may have been there for a long time.

Some problems can have three stones.

One for the past, how you used to feel about the problem.

One for how it affects you now.

And one for the future about anxieties you might have about what it may be like in the future.

Take your time.

Take all the time you need.

Stone by stone.

Some stones may have lost their labels.

Hard to remember what those stones represent.

But they still have weight so take them out and put them down by the door.

Some people have lots of stones.

Others only a few.

Some people even collect pebbles.

Each pebble is small.

Not very heavy.

But a lot of pebbles together can add up to a lot of weight.

Each pebble is probably too small for a label.

Too time consuming to unload individually.

So you can just tip any pebbles out at the end if they are there.

You can just raise your thumb when the backpack is emptied.

Now turn to the door.

Put your hand on the handle and go through the doorway into your special place.

The door closes behind you.

Feel the sense of bliss in this special place.

Feel the sense of freedom.

Look around at the place you find yourself.

Can you describe this place to me?

Now go back to the door and leave your special place of bliss.

You can always go back there.

Perhaps go there to experience bliss every day.

I like to start my day with experiencing a few moments of bliss.

Now look at the stones lying beside the door.

These stones represent all your problems.

Past, present and even future.

Only you know what these stones represent.

Only you know how many stones there are.

At this point you might like me to wave a magic wand and make all the problems disappear.

But that's not possible.

That would be fantasy.

This is reality.

And you know that in reality there are some things that cannot change.

You cannot change the past.

You cannot change one minute of the past.

Not even one second of the past.

In the same way you cannot change the stones.

You cannot change the size, the shape, the colour, the texture or the number of stones.

These cannot be changed.

But there is one really important change that you can make.

It is so simple yet can be so awesome.

You can change the location of the stones.

If you want, for some or even for all of the stones, you could choose to leave the stones lying there.

They would still be the same size, shape colour and texture as before.

But if you left the problem lying there, on the floor you would not be able to feel the weight any more.

This would turn the problem into a technicality.

Just a mere technicality.

You wouldn't be able to experience the feeling of weight any more.

Does that make sense?

On the other hand if for whatever reason you feel a need to carry some or even all of the stones as a burden then feel free to pick up those stones and put them in the backpack.

To experience the problems as a burden you need to be able to feel the weight of the problem ....
Does that make sense?

Can you appreciate the difference between a burden and a technicality?

Then carefully make your choice for each and every stone.

You don't have to decide for the rest of your life.

Just for today.

Are there any stones that you don't need to carry as a burden for the rest of today?

If so you can leave them there.

It's quite safe.

These are flat stones.

They won't roll away.

They will still be the same problems.

They will still have the same size, the same shape, the same texture, the same colour.

But you can now choose whether to carry the weight.

You cannot change your problems.

But you can choose whether you regard them as burdens or as technicalities ....

Take your time and choose.

It's awesome................................

When you have made your choice for the location of each stone, again in absolute privacy, then you can let me know by raising your thumb once more.

Now put the backpack on your back and start walking along the corridor.

See the doors to the right and the left.

And on the floor you may see some stones.

Some people are what I call "habitual stone picker-uppers."

No one is a born stone picker-upper.

You have to learn it.

Usually you learn it from a parent.

9 times out of 10 it's a mother you learn it from.

"Oh, there's a stone.

Be a good boy/girl and pick it up."

Lots of messages about "ought to" and "should."

I'm sure you know what I mean by that.

I've got a mother like that.

Many of us have mothers like that.

But some people with a lot of stones are not habitual stone picker-uppers.

They are usually very generous people.

Warm hearted and giving.

They sometimes leave their backpacks wide open and this allows other people or events, but particularly other people, to dump some of <u>their</u> stones in our backpack.

And I'm sure you know what I mean by that!

I got the idea for this exercise from a song that was popular in the 60's called 'Turn, Turn, Turn'.

You might remember the song, written by Pete Seeger and sung by a group called The Byrds, then later covered by The Seekers.

"There is a season, turn, turn, turn, and a time for everything under heaven……"

There is a line in the second verse of the song that says, "A time for laying down of stones, a time for gathering stones together."

(*Not the true lyrics—they say 'cast away stones'.*)

It suddenly occurred to me that 'stone gatherers' was a fairly good way of describing the people who come here with all sorts of problems that they have accumulated over the years.

Some have become quite skilled and seasoned stone gatherers.

But it's as if they have forgotten the first part of the verse.

There's a time for laying down of stones!

I wanted to write to Pete Seeger to thank him for the inspiration for this idea, till someone pointed out that he didn't write most of the words.

He used them.

The words of the song were not written in the 60's but in fact come from the Bible.

These words of the song are taken from the Book of Ecclesiastes, Chapter One.

Now I don't know what the original writer meant by those words but I think the original writer would be happy with your modern-day use of these words.

You can choose when it is your time to lay down your stones.

Each day you can lay down your stones and experience your special place of bliss.

Each day you can choose the location of your stones.

Even if you feel obliged to pick them all up again you can still be refreshed by spending time in the place of bliss without any burdens.

Some days you may be able to leave all the stones lying on the floor as mere technicalities.

On those days you can then start your day with a clear mind.

You can repeat this exercise in your own time as often as you wish.

I like to do it each morning.

Each time will be different.

You will learn something new each time you do.

You know, this exercise reminds me of an old joke in real estate.

What are the three most important factors in real estate?

They are location, location and location.

It is not the meaning of the stone that is most important.

It is not the size or the shape or the number.

It is not even the weight of the stones.

The three most important factors in determining whether any problem, any stone, is an intolerable burden or just a mere technicality are location, location and location.

You can start each day with a sense of bliss.

You can lay down your stones.

In so doing you can convert your burdens into technicalities.

But for now just gradually reorient yourself to this room and to this time.

Hear the noises around you more clearly and when you are ready just gradually open your eyes and come out of trance."

CHAPTER TEN

SPECIAL PLACE OF BLISS
MICRO-ANALYSIS

Today I'd like to teach you how to experience your very own unique special place of bliss……..	Pause
I'd like you to imagine a corridor.	Visualise
As you walk along the corridor there are doors leading off to the left and to the right.	These doors can be numbered and used in a subsequent session if desired as each number relates to a year in their life and behind that door there is a book and a visual representation of their life in that year
And at the end of the corridor see a door.	Visualise
A very inviting sort of door.	'Inviting' is an unusual adjective for a door but essential to avoid possible abreaction. People want to enter an inviting door. Never suggest a colour, you do not know if a particular colour could generate an unwanted memory, always let them choose.)
You can decide for yourself the size and shape of the door.	Comparable options—choice

Tell me, what colour is the door?

Wait for an answer to each of this and the following questions

Is the door a plain door or does it have panels?

Does the door have a handle?

Is the handle on the left or on the right?

What colour and shape is the handle?

Now look very closely, does the door seem to open inwards or outwards?

Answering these questions establishes that the subject is actively visualizing a particular door. Imagining a door is not a difficult task for anyone and if someone claims to be unable to see a door then do NOT proceed. This is a sign of resistance and probably means that that the person has some concerns about the safety of the planned procedure. I have only ever had one person claim to be unable to imagine a door despite using this exercise with several thousand patients. She had aphantasia. In fact with that person I complimented their subconscious defence mechanisms that made them unable to visualise a simple door given that they obviously knew what a door was)

You may be wondering about this door?

About what lies behind the door?

In a few minutes you will discover that behind the door is a special place.

Nonspecific

Special Place of Bliss Micro-Analysis

Your very own special place.	Unique
A place that your imagination is already creating for you.	You do not have to be consciously aware of it now
It is a special place.	
A place of bliss.	
Absolute bliss!	
Now bliss is an old-fashioned word.	Truism
It's not used much nowadays.	Truism
Let me be quite clear about what I mean by bliss.	
Bliss is a state of mind.	Truism
Bliss is far more than just the absence of negativities.	Truism
The absence of worries, the absence of problems, concerns, difficulties, traumas and upsets.	Truism
Bliss is more than that.	Truism
As well as the absence of negativities, bliss is also the positive presence of such concepts as freedom, peace, comfort, joy, happiness, relaxation and rest.	Helpful suggestion spoken as if every word is also a truism
Absolute pleasure.... sheer.....bliss.	
So, in order to experience a sense of bliss then we have to, at least on a temporary basis, be able to put all of our problems and worries and concerns off to one side.	Another helpful suggestion said as a truism
So, on your back you will find a backpack.	This is a handy segue or link word even when there is no obvious linkage

171

Take the backpack off and place it in front of you.	Direct suggestion
Open the backpack.	Direct suggestion
Inside you will find a collection of stones.	
Special stones.	
Notice how the stones are somewhat flat, but rounded and smooth, rather like the sort of stones you might find on the bed of a river or a rocky beach perhaps.........	
Do you see the special stones?	Wait for confirmation
These stones are special because in hypnosis they are very symbolic.	
The stones represent <u>all</u> of your particular problems.	
<u>Every</u> problem.	
<u>Every</u> concern.	That's a particularly important reframe
And because these stones represent <u>every</u> problem, not just the ones that you have told me about.	
I want to make one thing <u>clear</u>.	
This next part of the exercise will be carried out in <u>total and absolute</u> privacy.	Reassurance
Now by total and absolute privacy I don't just simply mean the normal confidentiality that you would expect and will of course receive from a doctor.	Further reassurance

Special Place of Bliss Micro-Analysis

No, I mean far more than that.	Even better
By total and absolute privacy I mean that you will do the next part of the exercise entirely inside your own head, in silence.	No disclosure
So that only you will ever know what particular issues these stones represent for you.	
Let me be absolutely clear.	Further reassurance
I will never, ever, ask you to talk about the meaning of your stones.	Unvoiced 'therefore'
Only you will ever know how many stones are in the backpack.	
Again I will never, ever ask you to talk about the number of stones.	
And perhaps most importantly of all only you will ever know the weight of each particular stone.	
Obviously the weight of the stones relates to the weight of the problems.	A word that actually means 'it is not obvious' but makes the proposition sound self-evident
Again I will never, ever ask you to talk about the weight of any of the stones.	
Is that guarantee of privacy completely understood?	Wait for a nod or other indication of confirmation of understanding of complete privacy
These stones represent all of the problems that you have in your mind.	
There are the problems of now, the present.	

The issues and concerns that are on your mind now, today, this very day.

But there are also stones about the past.

And the past includes yesterday, last week, last month, last year, ten years ago, many years ago.

All the way back to your earliest memories of problems from childhood.

And there can also be stones from the future.

How can this be since the future hasn't happened yet?

Well, these are what I call the "What if?" stones.

Some people carry around stones that represent worries about what might happen in the future.

Did I not say, 'All worries?'

What could go wrong!

What might not change!

Exclamations and not questions

Sometimes these stones are possibilities.

Sometimes remote possibilities.

But some people carry them around like rocks of probabilities.

Or even as huge boulders of certainties.

Alliteration

Your imagination will tell you what size each stone and issue is.

Quantification and naming will happen automatically

Now look at the stones in the backpack.	Visualise
This is what I want you to do.	Listen carefully
In a few moments I will give you the signal to start safely emptying the backpack.	
This is how I want you to empty it.	Instructions coming up
In a moment I want to you look at the top stone.	
It will probably have a label on it.	(It may not!)
To let you know what problem it represents.	
I want you to read the label and identify the problem.	
Then, briefly, pick up the stone and feel the weight of the stone and then place it down on the floor beside the door.	Briefly is particularly important to avoid any possible abreaction!
Then turn to the backpack and identify the next stone, feel the weight of that stone and then put it down beside the door.	
Keep doing this till the backpack is completely empty.	
Then when you have taken the time you need to completely empty your backpack you can let me know that it is empty by raising your right thumb in the air.	
Are those instructions clear?	Wait for some sign of confirmation
Then turn to the backpack and now start unloading all your problems	

Stone by stone ....

Issue by issue ....

Problem by problem ....

Till the bag is completely empty.

Take all the time you need.   Within reason

Give the person time to empty their stones.

A few useful interjections every so often can be helpful.

E.g. Some of the stones are the ones you expected to find there.

Others might be a bit of a surprise.

Some of the stones may be heavier than you had expected.

Some may be surprisingly light.

Some of the stones may have been there for a long time.

Some problems can have three stones.

One for the past, how you used to feel about the problem.

One for how it affects you now.

And one for the future about anxieties you might have about what it may be like in the future.

Take your time.

Take all the time you need.

Stone by stone.

Special Place of Bliss Micro-Analysis

Some stones may have lost their labels.	That's OK to not remember
Hard to remember what those stones represent.	
But they still have weight so take them out and put them down by the door.	Even forgotten burdens can be put down
Some people have lots of stones.	
Others only a few.	Truisms
Some people even collect pebbles.	
Each pebble is small.	
Not very heavy.	
But a lot of pebbles together can add up to a lot of weight.	Truism
Each pebble is probably too small for a label.	
Too time consuming to unload individually.	
So you can just tip any pebbles out at the end if they are there.	Easy to deal with
You can just raise your thumb when the backpack is emptied.	When the thumb eventually rises then proceed to the next phase.
Now turn to the door.	
Put your hand on the handle and go through the doorway into your special place.	
The door closes behind you.	
Feel the sense of bliss in this special place.	

Feel the sense of freedom.	Kinaesthetic/emotional suggestion
Look around at the place you find yourself.	Visualisation suggestion
Can you describe this place to me?	Utilise whatever imagery is reported and interpret it in the most blissful way. Let the person spend a couple of minutes experiencing a sense of blissfulness
Now go back to the door and leave your special place of bliss.	
You can always go back there.	To address any sadness at leaving
Perhaps go there to experience bliss every day.	
I like to start my day with experiencing a few moments of bliss.	A shared experience
Now look at the stones lying beside the door.	
These stones represent all your problems.	
Past, present and even future.	Truism
Only you know what these stones represent.	
Only you know how many stones there are.	Truism
At this point you might like me to wave a magic wand and make all the problems disappear.	
But that's not possible.	

That would be fantasy.	
This is reality.	Really? Hypnosis is reality?
And you know that in reality there are some things that cannot change.	Truism
You cannot change the past.	Truism
You cannot change one minute of the past.	Truism
Not even one second of the past.	Truism
In the same way you cannot change the stones.	Truism
You cannot change the size, the shape, the colour, the texture or the number of stones.	Truism
These cannot be changed.	Truism
But there is one really important change that you can make.	
It is so simple yet can be so awesome.	
You can change the location of the stones.	Truism
If you want, for some or even for all of the stones, you could choose to leave the stones lying there.	Truism
They would still be the same size, shape, colour and texture as before.	Truism
But if you left the problem lying there, on the floor you would not be able to feel the weight any more.	Truism
This would turn the problem into a technicality.	

Just a mere technicality.	Said with a dismissive tone
You wouldn't be able to experience the feeling of weight any more.	Truism
Does that make sense?	Wait for confirmation and give clarification if needed
On the other hand if for whatever reason you feel a need to carry some or even all of the stones as a burden then feel free to pick up those stones and put them in the backpack.	I usually give a slight sigh of disbelief)
	Having a burden is thus a chosen option
To experience the problems as a burden you need to be able to feel the weight of the problem	
………………………………….. Does that make sense?	
Can you appreciate the difference between a burden and a technicality?	Wait for confirmation
Then carefully make your choice for each and every stone.	No rush
You don't have to decide for the rest of your life.	
Just for today.	
Are there any stones that you don't need to carry as a burden for the rest of today?	This is the most important message
If so, you can leave them there.	
It's quite safe.	Reassurance
These are flat stones.	
They won't roll away.	Truism

Special Place of Bliss Micro-Analysis

They will still be the same problems.	Truism
They will still have the same size, the same shape, the same texture, the same colour.	Truisms
But you can now choose whether to carry the weight.	Helpful suggestion
You cannot change your problems.	(Truism)
But you can choose whether you regard them as burdens or as technicalities	
Take your time and choose.	
It's awesome	'It" is undefined
When you have made your choice for the location of each stone, again in absolute privacy, then you can let me know by raising your thumb once more.	Wait till the thumb rises
Now put the backpack on your back and start walking along the corridor.	
See the doors to the right and the left.	Reversing the laterality
And on the floor, you may see some stones.	Possibility
Some people are what I call "habitual stone picker-uppers."	You might be such a person
No one is a born stone picker upper.	
You have to learn it.	It's not genetic
Usually you learn it from a parent.	
9 times out of 10 it's a mother you learn it from.	

"Oh, there's a stone. Be a good boy/girl and pick it up."	Use appropriate gender of the patient
Lots of messages about "ought to" and "should."	
I'm sure you know what I mean by that.	
I've got a mother like that.	Shared upbringing
Many of us have mothers like that.	It's common
But some people with a lot of stones are not habitual stone picker-uppers.	
They are usually very generous people.	
Warm hearted and giving.	
They sometimes leave their backpacks wide open and this allows other people or events, but particularly other people, to dump some of <u>their</u> stones in our backpack.	Pause—for two seconds
And I'm sure you know what I mean by that!	
I got the idea for this exercise from a song that was popular in the 60's called 'Turn, Turn, Turn'.	
You might remember the song, written by Pete Seeger and sung by a group called The Byrds, then later covered by The Seekers.	
"There is a season, turn, turn, turn, and a time for everything under heaven......"	

There is a line in the second verse of the song that says, "A time for laying down of stones, a time for gathering stones together."

Not the true lyrics—they say—cast away stones

It suddenly occurred to me that 'stone gatherers' was a fairly good way of describing the people who come here with all sorts of problems that they have accumulated over the years.

Some have become quite skilled and seasoned stone gatherers.

But it's as if they have forgotten the first part of the verse.

There's a time for laying down of the stones!

I wanted to write to Pete Seeger to thank him for the inspiration for this idea, till someone pointed out that he didn't write most of the words.

He used them.

The words of the song were not written in the 60's but in fact come from the Bible.

These words of the song are taken from the Book of Ecclesiastes, Chapter One.

Now I don't know what the original writer meant by those words but I think the original writer would be happy with your modern-day use of these words.

You can choose when it is your time to lay down your stones.

You have a choice

Each day you can lay down your stones and experience your special place of bliss.

Each day you can choose the location of your stones.

Even if you feel obliged to pick them all up again you can still be refreshed by spending time in the place of bliss without any burdens.

Some days you may be able to leave all the stones lying on the floor as mere technicalities.

On those days you can then start your day with a clear mind.

You can repeat this exercise in your own time as often as you wish.

I like to do it each morning.   I also use this technique

Each time will be different.

You will learn something new each time you do.

You know, this exercise reminds me of   Light comedy
an old joke in real estate.

What are the three most important factors in real estate?

They are location, location and location.

It is not the meaning of the stone that is most important.

It is not the size or the shape or the number.

It is not even the weight of the stones.	
The three most important factors in determining whether any problem, any stone, is an intolerable burden or just a mere technicality are location, location and location.	Link to the comedy
You can start each day with a sense of bliss.	
You can lay down your stones.	
In so doing you can convert your burdens into technicalities.	
But for now just gradually reorient yourself to this room and to this time.	Reorientation
Hear the noises around you more clearly and when you are ready just gradually open your eyes and come out of trance.	Reassuring coming back to reality

SUMMARY

This combination brief therapy septet of the Structured Anxiety Intake Session, The Teapot Test, The Magnifying Glass Metaphor, The Four Finger Technique, the Silly Voice Metaphor, the How to Think Like an Optimist session and the Special Place of Bliss may not always cure all your patients with Anxiety or Panic but will certainly cure most of them and will certainly be of help to everyone. I would go even further and ask how it would ever be possible to cure anxiety in anyone without the patient learning how to control their autonomic nervous system and produce rapid relaxation, displace and replace their unwanted thoughts, learn how to recognise truths from lies, know how to think like an optimist and be able to park all of their emotional baggage and never carry it again.

Only I however can deliver these words above with authenticity and conviction but I hope you adapt and modify these words to suit your own practice. The detailed micro-analysis should certainly assist you to write hypnosis scripts of your own. These methods mentioned above are but seven of the fifty or more modules of therapy I commonly use in practice.

I like to think of my style of therapy as Modular Hypnosis and these seven modules work well for people presenting with Anxiety or Panic. Every other condition I see has a typical standard intake session e.g. for insomnia or chronic pain, followed usually by the magnifying glass metaphor then two or three other modules specific to the presenting problem.

These four techniques above are ways to address the Experiential Deficits that result in them having what I call Emotional Illiteracy which happens to be my term for Anxiety and Panic.

If someone cannot read and write it is fruitless to enquire about their schooling and seek to find reasons for their inability. It is far more useful to teach them how to read and write. That's why I do not ask my patients with anxiety why they cannot relax, cannot get rid of their unwanted thoughts, do not know how to be optimistic or deal with their emotional baggage. I see no reason to seek reasons for their inability to do these things. I know I can teach them these skills and that by listening to the recording of the session they can turn teaching into learning.

I have many other modules I have not covered and hopefully if this first therapy book is well received, I will probably write about how I treat several other problems.

ABOUT THE AUTHOR

I am a specialised generalist. I can use hypnosis and other techniques to treat A—Anxiety, B—Bulimia C—Chronic pain, D—Depression, E—Eating disorders and virtually all the other letters of the alphabet apart from Q. I do treat zoophobia!

That is typical of life in New Zealand. We are only 5,100,000 people in NZ and we need to be expert in many aspects of our work. There are not enough people in New Zealand to only practice in a narrow clinical niche.

I first attended a weekend hypnosis workshop and learned about the medical use of hypnosis in 1991. I was instantly hooked on hypnosis and was using it in my medical practice the very next day. By 1993 I was first elected President of the New Zealand Society of Hypnosis and in 1996 I opened the first ever medical hypnosis practice in New Zealand.

25 years later it is still the only medical hypnosis practice in NZ.

I've previously written two self help books, Relax: Say Goodbye to Anxiety and Panic and Quit: Say Goodbye to Smoking both published in New Zealand by Huia Publishers.

In November 2019 I had written the first version of this book and after giving a lecture in Heidelberg I was asked to have my early manuscript translated into German despite it never having been published in English before and so it was published as 'Wie man angst in nur vier therapiesitsungen heilt' by Carl-Auer Verlag and it had a glowing preface written by Bernhard Trenkle, the President of the International Society of Hypnosis. Apparently it is selling well. I do not speak or understand German however and cannot read the book. This is the first English language version of my ideas and the first to include the important lie detector chapter thus changing the title from 'just four therapy sessions' to 'just five'.

I have developed a unique style of hypnosis that combines some of the best elements from Classical Hypnosis, Ericksonian Hypnosis, Storytelling and Acting that has been simply dubbed by my peers as ……….

The McCarthy Methods

My methods certainly work for me and for the more than 15,000 people I have treated for anxiety or panic as of 2021. Almost no one who reads this book will have ever seen me treat a patient, yet I have been working in hypnosis and general practice since 1991. That's 30 years of working solo. There are only two people in my room usually. The patient and me. Sometimes parents of the patient with a young person. In a hospital surrounded by colleagues we usually learn how to work by observing our teachers. We learn what works and perhaps even more importantly what does not work. Yet as a therapist, after initial training we are left to develop our own style of working usually in isolation. My office suite for instance, contains seven rooms and there are seven therapists using each room. We might mingle for morning tea or lunch and perhaps share a cookery recipe but never a therapy recipe, and we never see each other

About the Author

working. I have no idea about their approach or treatment. I have no idea how they talk to a patient and what happens in any of their sessions. Watching a live demonstration with a volunteer subject from the audience at a conference given by an 'expert' is not the same as watching a genuine therapeutic clinical interaction. This book seeks to address this important issue. I have given you as much detail as possible of my methodology so you can see the therapeutic strategy that works for me but I cannot possibly convey in print the real essence of a consultation with Dr Patrick McCarthy. You do not see my genuine smile, feel my handshake, or register the twinkle in my eyes as I warmly greet each patient in my soft Scottish accent as though they were the most important person in my life at that moment. You do not see me convert their curiosity and desperation into hope and expectancy. What other textbook on anxiety that you have ever read starts with a joke about a drunk man (which you can probably still remember) and contains acting instructions? For most of human history till the last couple of hundred years, doctors and 'medicine men' and healers had no reliable therapeutics and the main therapy was the interaction between the patient and the healer. The word 'placebo' means 'I will please'. Successful therapists gave their patients hope and expectancy. We live in an age of a pill for each ill. The role of a modern doctor is often merely to select the correct pill. This book is about the art of being a true healer and a hope and expectancy generator.

As you may remember I wrote earlier but it is worth repeating

People with anxiety are also like a large box of chocolates. Every single chocolate in the box may well have a unique colour of wrapper just as every patient with anxiety has a unique personal story but underneath the wrapper you will always find a chocolate that contains cocoa, butter, sugar and a flavouring. With anxiety you will always find sympathetic overactivity (Use the Magnifying Glass Metaphor), mistaken thoughts (Use the Four Finger technique), making the mistake of believing them (The Silly Voice Metaphor) and pessimistic thinking (The 3P's). Instead of obsessing about and feeling the need to understand every detail of the wrapping I believe it is far more important to focus on negating all the ingredients ALWAYS there. The wrapper (the emotional baggage) is not completely unimportant of course but what if that can always be scrunched up and discarded (The Special Place of Bliss) and no longer carried with no need for discussion.

My hope is you can appreciate which aspects of these techniques and approaches can be adapted and incorporated into your own therapeutic style and approach to improve your ability to use hypnosis to cure anxiety and panic in your patients. That's just a suggestion after all.

CPSIA information can be obtained
at www.ICGtesting.com
Printed in the USA
BVHW051652200423
662741BV00009B/376